Stories With Scriptures
Devotionals for Young Readers

Light
for your
Path

Mary Ellen Beachy

Illustrated by:
Coleen Barnhart

Vision Publishers
HARRISONBURG, VA

Light for Your Path
ISBN 1-932676-10-4
© 1999 Mary Ellen Beachy
© 2008 Vision Publishers

First Edition 1999
Second Printing 2002
Second Edition 2008

All Scripture quotations are from the King James Version of the Holy Bible.

COPYRIGHTS
"Safe in the Arms of Jesus," Fanny J. Crosby, 1868, public domain, page 23.
"Tragedy at the Dance," as told to the author by LeRoy Beachy, page 140.
"The Boy Who Cried Wolf," attributed to Aesop, 620-560 B.C., page 212.
"Mansion Over the Hilltop," Ira Forest Stanphill, 1949, New Spring Publishing,
  used by permission, page 124.
"My Bible and I," Harry Dixon Loes, public domain, page 90.
"God Will Take Care of You," Civilla D. Martin, 1945, public domain, page. 57.
"All Night, All Day," public domain, spiritual, page 46.
"I'll Be a Sunbeam," public domain, Gospel Publishers, page 30.
"Hallelujah Square," Benson Company, public domain, page 14.
"The Little Lamb," American Bible Society, December 1995, pages 19-22.
"I Love You, Mother," New Educational Readers Book II, 1900, page 4.
  Stories about Tan from the book Tan by Florence Faviss, pages 80-87.
"I Want a Bike" and "It Would Not Burn," The Angel's Message, Life Ministries, pages 98, 132.
  Nancy Coblentz, missionary in Belize, page 162.
"Sanctuary," Michael Cohn, 1982, TKO Group, page 159.

Cover and Text Design: Lonnie D. Yoder
Editors: Timothy Kennedy, John D. Risser, Shannon Latham and others

For additional copies or comments write to:
Vision Publishers
P.O. Box 190
Harrisonburg, VA 22803
Fax: 540/437-1969.
Phone: 877/488-0901
E-mail: orders@vision-publishers.com
www.vision-publishers.com
(see order form in back)

Dedicated to My Mother

NAOMI K. STOLTZFUS

Like the faithful beams of
the lighthouse rays,
Your love and prayers
Bless all my days.

Countless are the hours
While on your knee
Character-building stories
You read to me.

Thank you, Mother, for your godly example.

For our children:
*Mary, Margretta, Matthias, Marcellus,
Markus, and Micah*
I have no greater joy than to hear that my children walk in truth.
—3 John 4

Acknowledgments

I owe my gratitude to
my husband Mark
for encouraging me in my writing and for
the hours he spent typing
the original manuscript.

Introduction

The eastern sky was filled with gorgeous hues of pink and red. Mark stood by the window admiring the lovely sunrise. "What a beautiful morning!" he softly exclaimed.

The house was quiet; all six children were still asleep.

Mark knelt to pray. Prayer and Bible reading every morning were as routine to him as eating breakfast. He sought wisdom and help from God to lead and shepherd his family along the narrow road that leads to life and heaven.

While he prayed, he heard the old stairway creak. A small pajama-clad figure was slowly coming down the steps, rubbing the sleep from his eyes. He saw his father praying. Quickly he ran to his father and snuggled right in under Daddy's strong arm. He felt so warm, secure, and loved as he knelt by his dad.

In this world of change, turmoil, and fear, children have many needs. But most of all, they need parents who walk with God and truly love the Lord. They need parents who with confidence can say to their children, "Follow me, as I follow Christ."

The psalmist David said that God's word "is more to be desired . . . than gold, yea, than much fine gold." He also said, "I love thy commandments, above gold; yea, above fine gold."

Have we as parents found that to be true in our lives?

The prayer of my heart is that the factual accounts in this book, coupled with Scriptures, will encourage our children to truly love the Word of God and to establish the habit of reading it every day.

Because of Jesus,

Mary Ellen Beachy

Contents

Dedication	3
Acknowledgements	5
Introduction	7
The Fruit of the Spirit	11
Sunbeams	41
Angels	57
Prayer and Words	71
Courage	85
The Word	101
For the Lord	117
Contentment	133
Consequences	151
Missionaries	169
The Ten Commandments	201
Virtues	229

The Bible is . . .

A wonderful treasure.

    1. Open it.
    2. Read it.
    3. Memorize it.
    4. Live it.

Its treasures will bless all your days.

The Fruit of the Spirit

The fruit of the Spirit in our lives is evidence that we love the Lord. Is this fruit a part of your life?

LOVE = affection and devotion evidenced by what we do.

JOY = gladness of heart. Jesus brings true joy in the heart.

PEACE = rest, ease, security. When we are at peace with God, we are live peaceably with others.

LONGSUFFERING or **PATIENCE** = sweetness of temper, bearing trials without murmuring, not losing your temper when things aggravate and irritate.

GENTLENESS = kindness, tenderness; not being severe, rough, or violent.

GOODNESS = caring about others, doing what is good.

FAITH = confidence and trust in God.

MEEKNESS = patient, gentle, kind, submissive, humble.

TEMPERANCE = self control; not being extreme in opinion, speech, or action. It is allowing Christ to control us.

. . . from a vine we look for grapes

. . . from an apple tree we look for apples

. . . from a Christian we look for the fruits of love, joy, and peace

To be fruitful we must abide in Jesus, walking and talking with Him daily.
The fruit of the Spirit in us honors God and cheers man.

Treasure Search

But the fruit of the Spirit is love, joy, peace, longsuffering, gentleness, goodness, faith, meekness, temperance: against such there is no law.

Galatians 5:22, 23

READ JOHN 15:1-5

Love

This is my commandment, That ye love one another, as I have loved you. ~John 15:12

My little children, let us not love in word, neither in tongue; but in deed and in truth. ~1 John 3:18

I LOVE YOU, MOTHER

Three children, Nell, Fannie, and Jack said they loved their mother. But one truly loved best of all!

Jack said, "Mother, I love you. I like to help you. I am a big strong boy. Let me get the water for you this morning." He went to get a pail of water from the well. Just then he saw some friends swinging in the garden. He forgot his work and ran to play. Mother had to bring in the water.

"Mother, I love you, too," said Nell. "You are such a good, dear mother. I will help you work. Let me bake a cake!"

"No, dear Nell," said Mother, "I will bake the cake. You help by getting eggs, flour, and spice for me."

Nell began to pout and fret. She wanted to bake the cake all by herself. It was miserable to have a grumbling girl in the house. Mother was glad when Nell ran out to play.

Fannie said, "I love you, Mother. I am glad I can help you work. I want to do something to show my love to my good, kind mother."

"Fannie," Mother said, "You may rock the baby." Once the baby was asleep, Fannie helped Mother sweep and dust. She was happy all day helping Mother. She worked with a song on her lips. When night came, Fannie went to bed a happy girl. Her love for her mother was true love.

What we do for others is the best test of love.

Treasure Search

Seeing ye have purified your souls in obeying the truth through the Spirit unto unfeigned love of the brethren, see that ye love one another with a pure heart fervently.

1 Peter 1:22

READ JOHN 3:16

Joy

Thou wilt shew me the path of life; in thy presence is fullness of joy; at thy right hand there are pleasures for evermore. ~Psalm 16:11

For the kingdom of God is not meat and drink; but righteousness, and peace, and joy in the Holy Ghost. ~Romans 14:17

SONGS AT MIDNIGHT

I can think of no better example of joy than the joy of Paul and Silas. They were falsely accused, beaten till their backs were bleeding, then put into an inner prison room with their feet firmly fastened in stocks.

What an uncomfortable position that must have been! Their backs were bruised and sore.

Wouldn't they just cry and complain? No, in the black of the darkness of the lonely midnight hour, they prayed and sang praises to their Lord in heaven. The other prisoners heard them. Had there ever before been joyful songs of praise in the prison?

Most important, God heard their prayers and songs. He was pleased with their faith and joy.

Suddenly there was a mighty, violent earthquake. The prison doors flew open, and the stocks fell off their feet.

The jailer was terrified when he awoke and saw all the open prison doors. He thought the prisoners had escaped. He was about to end his life when Paul called out, "Don't harm yourself, we are all here!"

That night they shared Jesus with the jailer and his family. The jailer washed their backs and gave them food. He believed in Jesus and rejoiced, because Paul and Silas had trusted God to care for them.

Taken from Acts 16:19–34

How blest are those who have peace and joy in Jesus in the midst of trials.

Treasure Search

Your heart shall rejoice, and your joy no man taketh from you.

John 16:22

READ ROMANS 15:13

Peace

Wherefore, beloved, seeing that ye look for such things, be diligent that ye may be found of him in peace, without spot, and blameless. –2 Peter 3:14

A SOFT ANSWER

Two little girls were playing with dolls together. The older girl had a beautiful new doll in her arms. The younger girl became jealous, crept up softly behind her, and gave her sister a sharp slap on her cheek.

A visitor sitting in another room saw what happened. She expected the big girl to slap her little sister back. But she didn't. She briefly looked upset as she rubbed her cheek with one hand and held her doll more closely. Then in a gentle tone she said, "Oh, Sallie, I didn't think you'd do that!" Sallie looked ashamed but said nothing. "Here, Sallie," her sister continued, "Sit in my chair and I'll let you hold my doll, if you'll be very careful."

Sallie reached for the doll. She was surprised at her big sister's kindness and gave her a glance of appreciation mingled with shame.

The visitor was amazed and surprised that a child could be so calm and forgiving when slapped. She called the girl over to her and asked, "How can you be so patient with Sallie?"

"Oh," she laughed, "I guess it's because I love my sister so much. She has a bad temper and forgets herself. Mama said if I should do angry things back to her we'd have a dreadful time and end up fighting and hurting each other. 'Learn to give the soft answer,' Mama said, and I'm trying to."

The lady kissed the girl and said, "My dear, I think you have learned that lesson!"

Jesus helps us live in peace.

Treasure Search

A soft answer turneth away wrath;
but grievous words stir up anger.

Proverbs 15:1

READ ROMANS 12:18 AND JOHN 14:27

Longsuffering
or Patience

Be ye also patient; stablish your hearts: for the coming of the Lord draweth nigh. ~James 5:8

A merry heart doeth good like a medicine; but a broken spirit drieth the bones. ~Proverbs 17:22

Where do we need more patience than with those we live with and love the best? At home, parents react to things that happen with love, patience, and humor, or with impatience and unkindness.

A TEST OF PATIENCE

The dirty supper dishes from the night before were still in the sink. Piles of laundry were waiting to be done. The little girls needed to have their hair combed. There were diapers to be changed, shoes to tie, children to feed, and stories to read.

The dirty breakfast dishes and cereal were still on the table. The baby needed to be rocked to sleep.

Meanwhile, my busy two-year-old decided it was time for more cereal. He climbed up on a chair and poured his little red bowl full of granola. It was so heaping full, it ran over and was dribbling down to the floor. Later, I went out to the kitchen. The little boy with all the cereal was disgusting, yet funny.

"Girls," I called, "come and look what Matthias did." They came running. We all looked and laughed together.

The children were happy because I was happy.

A merry heart brightens any day!

Treasure Search

Now the God of patience and consolation grant you to be likeminded one toward another according to Christ Jesus.
Romans 15:5

READ LUKE 21:19 AND HEBREWS 10:36

Gentleness

And the servant of the Lord must not strive; but be gentle unto all men, apt to teach, patient. –2 Timothy 2:24

A MOTHER'S LOVE

The morning sunshine streamed warmly through David's bedroom window, filling his room with its golden light. His mother Lydia came in. "Good morning, David," she said as she bent to kiss his cheek. "Arise, shine, for your light has come, and the glory of the Lord has risen upon you."

Tenderly, she dressed her son. He didn't respond with sweet baby coos and happy giggles as she carried him to the table and set him on his chair to feed him.

When David was born, he appeared to be a normal baby. But, when he was five days old, he wouldn't eat or drink anymore. He was yellow with jaundice. The doctor sent him to a specialist in Baltimore. Something was very wrong. They tried but could not help David.

Over the years, Lydia and her husband Amos took David to various doctors. At one time, they got family and friends to help with physical therapy. Finally there was nothing else to try. David would be helpless until God called him home.

Lydia is no longer a mother, she is a grandmother. David is not a small child. Yet every day, for 35 years now, she has gently cared for his needs: feeding, bathing, singing for him, and reciting poetry. David is helpless, he cannot talk, sing, or walk. He is totally dependent on his parents.

Lydia is my aunt. She has graciously, uncomplainingly accepted David's handicaps. She is thankful he isn't a wayward son. She is diligent, loves to work, and helps others. "If you wait to help others till it suits perfectly you won't get it done," she says. Her happiness comes from a heart in tune with God.

In heaven some sweet day, David will surely thank his mother for all her gentle loving care. Aunt Lydia's faithfulness will be rewarded.

Allow the disappointments in life to draw you nearer to God.

Treasure Search

But we were gentle among you,
even as a nurse cherisheth her children.

1 Thessalonians 2:7

READ 2 SAMUEL 22:36 AND JAMES 3:17

Gentleness

Continued

He Did What He Could

EPILOGUE TO DAVID'S STORY

On January 6, 1997, a cold winter morning, David's tired heart stopped beating. He was thirty-five years old.

The verse his mother has so often lovingly quoted for him became a wondrous reality for David: "Arise, shine, for thy light is come and the glory of the Lord is risen upon thee." —Isaiah 60:1

At his funeral, Johnny Stoltzfus, a cripple, sang a touching solo:

> I'll see all my friends in Hallelujah Square,
> What a wonderful time we'll all have up there.
> We'll sing and praise Jesus,
> His glory to share,
> And you'll not see one cripple in Hallelujah Square.

David is buried in a small country cemetery near Kennedyville, Maryland. His tombstone states simply: "God Gives Peace."

This statement echoes the confidence that ruled Lydia's heart all through David's life.

David's sister Anne wrote the following poem and read it at his funeral.

TO DAVID
FROM YOUR BROTHERS AND SISTERS
by Anne Yoder

Most of our children stay babies
    For only a few short years,
But David, you always needed your mother's arms
    And her comfort through sickness and tears.

To love you usually was easy.
    Automatically we gathered around you.
Whether it was eating, singing, playing;
    The right place was just to surround you.

At first we kept thinking of ways
    That maybe would help you to walk.
We wanted to know how you felt.
    We wanted to hear you talk.

We all enjoyed finding methods
    Of making you laugh and smile.
We'd put on records and sing songs for you
    Or read stories for pastime awhile.

We remember when you wouldn't miss chore time,
    And you always helped grind cow feed.
You sat outside and watched us fill silo,
    And enjoyed being there for each deed.

We loved to watch those expressive eyes.
    We were sure you knew more than you told us,
So we told you our secrets and had so much fun,
    Because you would just grin and make no fuss.

One of the most helpful things
    That ever came our way
Was when Angel's Haven opened their doors
    And said you could come every day.

You learned to know wonderful people
    As different ones came and went—
The bus drivers, the people who fed you,
    The many who generously spent.

They helped to make you comfortable;
    To your life they added so much.
The encouragement they gave us all
    Was such a loving touch.

And we haven't forgotten the years
    When extensive therapy was tried.
How we worked together to work you!
    And gave hours and hours at your side.

You were also a special blessing
  To our children as they came along.
The nephews and nieces just loved you.
  They combed your hair, gave drinks, sang songs.

Many people knew you were special.
  Some talked about the sunshine you brought,
While others so faithfully prayed
  And filled in when help was sought.

So for thirty-five years you changed our lives.
  You taught us compassion, togetherness.
You taught us about understanding the needs
  Of unfortunate ones who have less.

And for thirty-five years you always knew
  The care of a loving mother.
She sang to you, talked to you, fed you.
  And never complained to another.

But this last year was long and difficult.
  We think that you had much pain.
Your body seemed worn and tired,
  And you suffered time and again.

So Thursday when you slipped away,
  We were there to see you go.
We said, "Thank you, Lord," for this change,
  That is for your best, we know.

We thought of you being ushered
    Into heaven on feet that could walk.
We thought of the freedom from pain
    And of how you could laugh and talk.

Safe in the arms of Jesus
    Is where you now can stay.
Our family is started in heaven;
    We'll join you there some day.

Goodness

The Little Lamb

And whoso shall receive one such little child in my name receiveth me. ~Matthew 18:5

Take heed that ye despise not one of these little ones; for I say unto you, that in heaven their angels do always behold the face of my Father which is in heaven. ~Matthew 18:10

The doctors and nurses of Uberaba Children's Hospital in Brazil will always remember the day when little Silvania was brought into the emergency room. She was suffering from painful open sores on her face and body.

Nurse Graciete Nogueira and the staff were shocked at the three-year-old's behavior and bad language. How could such a young child use such bad words and swear so freely?

Her medical history sheet showed that she had been born and raised in a local brothel. Silvania was just copying the language she heard there every day.

A doctor and Nurse Graciete gently and patiently examined the little girl. They took blood tests and found she was suffering from advanced leukemia. Treatment was immediately started; hopefully the disease could be arrested.

Nurse Graciete felt drawn to the little girl. She asked to be assigned to her case. She spent whatever time she could, even meal breaks, tenderly and patiently bathing her, gently brushing her hair, and putting fresh bandages on her sores. She told her stories from the Bible. As the little girl became more interested in the Lord, Graciete taught her to pray. Silvania soaked up the love and stories just like dry ground soaks up rain. Soon her behavior changed for the better and she began to feel more peaceful and at rest.

The staff decided to keep Silvania at the hospital. They did not want to return her to the evil environment of the brothel. In time the little girl called her nurse "Auntie." The treatments slowed the progress of her disease.

Silvania learned what it meant to trust others, to love and be loved. She became gentle and cooperative.

Take time to bless a child.

Treasure Search

But when Jesus saw it, he was much displeased, and said unto them, Suffer the little children to come unto me, and forbid them not: for of such is the kingdom of God.

Verily I say unto you, Whosoever shall not receive the kingdom of God as a little child, he shall not enter therein.

And he took them up in his arms, put his hands upon them, and blessed them. Mark 10:14–16

READ MATTHEW 25:40

Goodness

The Little Lamb
Continued

He shall feed his flock like a shepherd: he shall gather the lambs with his arm, and carry them in his bosom, and shall gently lead those that are with young. ~Isaiah 40:11

Nurse Graciete introduced Silvania to the 23rd Psalm. The little girl was fascinated by Auntie's explanation of how God sent His Son Jesus to be our Good Shepherd. She memorized Psalm 23 and came to love it.

Through the Bible Society, the nurse got a New Reader Scriptures booklet for Silvania. On the cover was a picture of a shepherd and his little lamb. The little girl treasured her gift and read it again and again. Happily she shared the story with anyone who would listen.

Several years later Silvania's condition began to worsen, and gradually she grew weaker. The doctors could do little to help her. Nurse Graciete spent every minute she could with Silvania.

One night Silvania awoke and said, "Good-bye, Auntie, I go to my Shepherd." She closed her eyes, and soon she drew her last breath.

Loving angels carried her gently home to her Good Shepherd.

The next day, when Nurse Graciete made over Silvania's bed, she was comforted by finding tucked safely under the pillow, the little girl's most prized possession, the well-worn Scripture booklet with the picture of a shepherd and his lamb on the cover.

Though she grieved the loss of the precious child who had touched her life, Nurse Graciete rejoiced that Silvania was with her Shepherd in heaven, where there is no more sickness, pain, or death.

A compassionate nurse showed Silvania the road to heaven.

Treasure Search

And God shall wipe away all tears from their eyes; and there shall be no more death, neither sorrow, nor crying, neither shall there be any more pain: for the former things are passed away.

Revelation 21:4

READ PSALM 23

Faith

But without faith it is impossible to please him: for he that cometh to God must believe that he is, and that he is a rewarder of them that diligently seek him. ~Hebrews 11:6

The long black hearse slowly drove down the lane. Floyd stood and watched it go. His gaze followed the hearse until it passed out of his sight, for in it was the body of his beloved wife Lill.

The last six months had not been easy as Lill's health gradually declined due to bone cancer. Just last night, Floyd and their four children had gathered around Lill's bed. They knew the end was near. When Lill drew her last breath, her husband and children were singing Safe in the Arms of Jesus. The parting was real. Oh, how they would miss their wife and mother! Their tears freely flowed.

Through it all, Floyd's love and faith in God remained strong. Right after the funeral, he was with a group of supportive friends: missionaries he had worked with in Belize. They were singing. Floyd, who had just buried his wife and companion of nearly thirty years, joined in the song, *I Am Thine for Service.*

I have made my choice to follow Christ each day. . . . I will never ask thee how, or when, or why for I've cast my lot with thee. Till the glory gates shall open by and by with a welcome home for me.

Thine for service when the days are drear; thine for service when the skies are clear; Yes, thine for service through the coming years. I am thine for service, Lord!

That night, alone in bed, although weary and sad, Floyd knew God still loved him and would see him through each day.

Faith is clinging to God through all of life's joys and sorrows.

Treasure Search

So then faith cometh by hearing,
and hearing by the word of God.

Romans 10:17

READ ACTS 14:22

Meekness

Who, when he was reviled, reviled not again; when he suffered, he threatened not; but committed himself to him that judgeth righteously. –1 Peter 2:23

THE BIG BLACK MAN

The tall black man ran his hands gently over the sides and back of a big horse. It was Booker T. Washington's favorite riding horse, and it had accidentally been peppered with shot.

"Just leave the horse be," said Dr. Carver, "It was only birdshot and barely punctured his skin."

Washington hesitated, then said apologetically, "I think I'll double-check and get the veterinarian from town to come and look at my horse yet."

The vet came and thoroughly examined the fine horse. "Hmm," he said, "just leave him be; it was only birdshot and barely punctured his skin."

Carver never changed his expression; he didn't bother to say, "See, I told you so!"

Once a lady asked Dr. Carver to come and look at her sick fruit trees. Later she saw a poor black man with a patched sweater and shapeless cap coming down the road, surely a handyman or beggar. So she called to him, "Want to earn fifty cents? My grass needs cutting."

Dr. Carver kept silent. He neatly mowed her grass all around the house. Then he knocked at the door and said, "Now, what seems to be the trouble with your peaches, Madam?"

Dr. Carver knew what it was to be hurt, rejected, and turned away because his skin was black, yet his life was a legacy of love and kindess to those in need. He did all he could to help his fellowman.

The epitaph on Dr. Carver's tombstone sums up his life so well.

> He could have added fortune to fame,
> But caring for neither
> He found happiness and honor
> In helping the world.
> —Source Unknown

How did Dr. Carver's life show that he was meek?

Treasure Search

He was oppressed, and he was afflicted, yet he opened not his mouth; he is brought as a lamb to the slaughter, and as a sheep before her shearers is dumb, so he openeth not his mouth.

Isaiah 53:7

READ PSALM 25:9 AND 1 PETER 3:4

Temperance

He that is slow to anger is better than the mighty; and he that ruleth his spirit than he that taketh a city. –Proverbs 16:32

TEACHERS NEED TEMPERANCE

It was a busy day in a little old schoolroom. Most of my students were hard at work, except Herman, one of the fifth graders. He poked and fiddled and wouldn't keep at his work. Then he started to disturb the other students though I had warned him to get to work. When we had spelling, I saw him copy someone else's words. That was the last straw.

"Herman," I said, "come up to my desk." I was going to punish him. But would you believe it, Herman dashed for the door! I quickly decided I could catch that boy, so I ran after him. The road was muddy. What a sight! Herman tore down the road with me in hot pursuit. I gained on him though, getting closer and closer. Herman was getting desperate. Beside the road was a big wide ditch nearly full of water. Herman took a leap into the ditch and stood chest deep in the middle of it. He had won the race and stood there grinning stupidly at me.

I did not want to teach the rest of the day with wet, muddy pants so I left Herman in the ditch and went back to school feeling foolish.

Too late I realized that teachers should not chase their students. Chasing them does not win their respect and obedience. I would have to talk to Herman's parents and see if we could work together to help Herman cooperate at school.

Each morning, ask God for wisdom for the day.

Treasure Search

He that hath no rule over his own spirit is like a city that is broken down, and without walls.

Proverbs 25:28

READ 1 CORINTHIANS 9:25

Sunbeams

Happy homes
need helpful hands

Sunbeams for Jesus

WHAT ARE SUNBEAMS?

They are little, beaming rays of light coming down from heaven. They chase away gloomy dark shadows and bring light, gladness, and cheer wherever they go.

Are You a Sunbeam?

1. Jesus wants me for a sunbeam,
To shine for Him each day;
In every way try to please Him,
At home, at school, at play.

Chorus: A sunbeam, a sunbeam,
Jesus wants me for a sunbeam,
A sunbeam, a sunbeam,
I'll be a sunbeam for Him.

2. Jesus wants me to be loving,
And kind to all I see;
Showing how pleasant and happy,
His little ones can be.

3. I'll be a sunbeam for Jesus,
I can if I but try;
Serving him moment by moment,
Then live with him on high.

What are some things you can do to be a sunbeam? If you wish, write down how you could be one this week.

1.

2.

3.

4.

Sunbeams make home a happy place to be.

Treasure Search

The Lord hath done great things for us; whereof we are glad.

Psalm 126:3

READ PROVERBS 15:3 AND PROVERBS 17:22

Daddy Sunbeam

I have written unto you, fathers, because ye have known him that is from the beginning. I have written unto you, young men, because ye are strong, and the word of God abideth in you, and ye have overcome the wicked one. ~1 John 2:14

Daddy Sunbeam likes to make his family happy. Here are some things he does: Daddy Sunbeam has time to pray, sing, and read the Bible with his children. He plays with his children, crawling around on the floor, giving them horseback rides. Sometimes he plays Memory or Chinese checkers with happy children.

Daddy Sunbeam really loves his wife. When she is extra tired, he mops the kitchen floor for her. Other times he'll say, "Come, children, let's go on a walk." Away they go, while Mother stays at home to rest in the hammock and to read.

One morning Daddy Sunbeam encouraged Mother to go to a special meeting for ladies at church. Not only that, he also said, "Do not do any of your cleaning. The children and I will do all the cleaning for you!" That surely made Mother feel special, and glad she had married such a sunbeam!

How did Daddy Sunbeam even know how to clean? Well, his mother said that years ago he had often helped her clean and do the vacuuming. So, when he was a boy, he was a sunbeam for his mom.

Daddy Sunbeam sure is a wonderful man!

Follow your daddy as he follows Christ.

Treasure Search

And, ye fathers, provoke not your children to wrath; but bring them up in the nurture and admonition of the Lord.

Ephesians 6:4

READ EPHESIANS 5:25 AND TITUS 2:6-8

Mama Sunbeam

Who can find a virtuous woman? For her price is far above rubies. ~Proverbs 31:10

Every wise woman buildeth her house. ~Proverbs 14:1

Mama Sunbeam awoke with a prayer on her lips and a song in her heart; a prayer because she needed God's help and wisdom each day, and a song for she loved the Lord so much and rejoiced in all His goodness and blessings to her.

She wanted to spend time alone reading the Bible and meditating in the morning, but Susie, her own little Sunbeam, woke early. She snuggled right beside her mama. After a while, they studied Susie Sunbeam's Sunday School lesson together and read a good story.

Mama Sunbeam wanted each of her children to love Jesus and the Bible, so they talked about God, read Bible stories, and learned Bible verses.

Mama Sunbeam loved Daddy Sunbeam very, very much. She wanted to please him with good food, a tidy house, and being his best friend.

She loved and enjoyed her children. Just the other evening three of her little Sunbeams were swinging in the hammock. They were happy, smiling, and enjoying a bedtime snack, while Mama was singing.

Sometimes it is very hard for Mama Sunbeam to be patient, helpful, and cheerful. Once Susie sweetly asked for a swing ride. Mama was busy getting ready for company and rather sharply said, "No!" Later she apologized to Susie.

Susie said, "You should rather ask God to help you." To be a true Sunbeam, Mama realized, she needs to say "I'm sorry" when she is unkind and impatient with her children.

Mama knows she can be a Sunbeam only when Jesus lives in her heart and she walks with Him each day!

What must be done, is best done cheerfully.

Treasure Search

I can do all things through Christ which strengtheneth me.

Philippians 4:13

READ TITUS 2:4, 5 AND PROVERBS 31:30

Sammy Sunbeam

Do all things without murmurings and disputings.
~Philippians 2:14

And be ye kind one to another, tenderhearted,
forgiving one another, even as God for Christ's
sake hath forgiven you. ~Ephesians 4:32

Sammy Sunbeam is just four years old. Some mornings his job is to wash the breakfast dishes. One morning he got right to work without a grumble. His little sunbeam made the kitchen bright and happy.

One morning Sammy Sunbeam was outside with his little brother. They were looking for the wheelbarrow for their mom. They ran all around the yard searching: out to the barn, and down by the trash pile. Little brother was left behind and started to cry. Sammy Sunbeam ran back to him, held his hand, and walked slowly with him.

Sammy Sunbeam is a good singer, too. When the family has devotions, he joins with his clear, sweet voice. Sometimes when riding in the car, he sings quietly alone.

Sunbeams remember not to grumble and to do their work cheerfully! Parents really appreciate cheerful, kind, helpful sunbeams.

God in heaven must be smiling when children are sunbeams.

Were you a sunbeam today?

Treasure Search

Finally, be ye all of one mind,
having compassion one of another,
love as brethren, be pitiful, be courteous.

1 Peter 3:8

READ 2 PETER 1:5–7

Susie Sunbeam

Rooted and built up in him, and stablished in the faith, as ye have been taught, abounding therein with thanksgiving. —Colossians 2:7

Susie Sunbeam came down the steps bright and early one morning. She was the family's early bird.

Cheerfully she told her mother, "Good morning!" Then she dressed for school and sat down to read till breakfast was ready. When her two-year-old brother woke up, Mother gave him to Susie Sunbeam. She very sweetly picked him up and showed him some pretty pictures, while Mother got breakfast on the table.

When she left for school Susie kissed her mother good-bye.

That day she was a sunbeam at school, giving her teacher a cheery "good morning" and remembering to say "thank you" and "please." She shared her cough drops with a friend who needed some.

That evening when Mother asked her to wash the dishes, she was Susie Sad. But later her Sunbeam came back because she surprised Mother and wiped the dishes too.

Mother told her dear little Susie that she was so pleased that Susie had wiped the dishes without being told to.

When Susie Sunbeam was tucked into bed that night, she prayed and recited verses with her mother.

Surely, sunbeams like Susie sleep sweetly.

Sunbeams bring sunshine to others every day.

Treasure Search

And whatsoever ye do, do it heartily, as to the Lord, and not unto men;

Knowing that of the Lord ye shall receive the reward of the inheritance: for ye serve the Lord Christ.

Colossians 3:23, 24

READ 1 CORINTHIANS 15:58

Four Little Sunbeams Sing

It is a good thing to give thanks unto the Lord, and to sing praises unto thy name, O most high. ~Psalm 92:1

But ye shall receive power, after that the Holy Ghost is come upon you: and ye shall be witnesses unto me both in Jerusalem, and in all Judaea, and in Samaria, and unto the uttermost part of the earth. ~Acts 1:8

On a very cold winter morning, I was extra busy doing the laundry and making bread. My four children were happily playing, or trying to help.

I was surprised when I heard a knock at the door. Who could it be? There stood two Jehovah's Witnesses. Because it was cold outside, I invited them in. They talked briefly and wanted to give me some literature. I told them we love the Lord, we love the Bible, and we are not interested in what they have to offer. "But," I said, "May we sing for you?" I called the children, and they came running. I asked them to help me sing. I held the baby, and we sang, "Jesus loves me, this I know . . . ," "I am going to a city, where the streets with gold are laid . . . ," and "Full of happiness, praise the Lord . . .".

They seemed to enjoy our little impromptu concert. They didn't say much and soon left. We went back to our work and play, with happy hearts that we could sing for Jesus!

*Those who want to praise God in heaven
must first be praising Him here.*

Treasure Search

The living, the living, he shall praise thee, as I do this day: the father to the children shall make known thy truth.

Isaiah 38:19

READ PSALM 71:8

Friends are Sunbeams

As we have therefore opportunity, let us do good unto all men, especially unto them who are of the household of faith. ~Galatians 6:10

"Let's have a tea party!" said Ruby. "I'll bring a tea party to your house tomorrow morning at 10:00."

And that is just what Ruby Sunbeam did! She came with delicious fresh fruit, sweet cream sticks, and dainty little tea cookies. We had a nice tea party on our front porch that summer morning, thanks to Ruby Sunbeam.

Alta Sunbeam came and brought extra warmth and cheer to our home on a cold winter evening. We had such a nice visit with our chairs pulled up close to the fireplace. She loved our children, too, and brought a pretty gift bag full of goodies and a present for each of our children. We sang together, went to church, and to a friend's house for lunch with this happy sunbeam!

Some sunbeams work together. Three families from one church get together to take a meal to a lonely widow or a sick person, or they invite the minister's family into their homes in a gesture of appreciation. They have learned that bringing cheer to others makes their lives brighter and happier.

Sunbeam friends are friends who like you, encourage you, and lighten your load.

Treasure Search

And the king said, Is there not yet any of the house of Saul, that I may shew the kindness of God unto him?

2 Samuel 9:3

READ 1 CORINTHIANS 16:18 AND PHILEMON 7

Angels

The angel of the Lord encampeth
round about them that fear him, and
delivereth them.   ~Psalm 34:7

Angels

All night, all day,
Angels watching over me, my Lord,
All night, all day,
Angels watching over me!

Three hundred and eleven verses in the Bible speak of angels. There is something mysterious about angels, likely because most of us have never seen angels.

Hebrews 1:14 calls angels ministering spirits. Angels are God's spirit messengers sent out to help and care for those who love the Lord.

In Bible times angels were sent by God to give people special messages.

People were frightened when they saw an angel. Maybe it was because they were shining brightly with the glory of the Lord. The angel would first tell them—"Fear not." God does not want His children to be afraid.

Matthew 18:10 talks about children and their angels. We like to call those angels guardian angels. Often we are protected from dangers of which we are not aware.

Thank God for His love and protection.

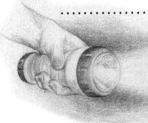

Treasure Search

But while he thought on these things, behold, the angel of the Lord appeared unto him in a dream, saying, Joseph, thou son of David, fear not to take unto thee Mary thy wife: for that which is conceived in her is of the Holy Ghost.

Matthew 1:20

READ LUKE 1:30 AND LUKE 2:10

Carried by Angels

Ervin Beachy had a prosperous farm and turkey barns in Ohio. He was a strong, cheerful, enthusiastic man who worked with a will. He had a heart of love and compassion for poor people and cared enough to offer them a helping hand.

He would fly to Haiti and work with missions there, doing what he could to help. Each year, he helped organize a huge auction to raise money for missionaries in Haiti. At one of the mission board meetings, he said he didn't think he'd ever go back to Haiti again. This surprised the other men, as Ervin had always enjoyed going.

In the wintertime, Ervin drove big truckloads of logs to a sawmill. One winter morning when he told his wife good-bye, she never dreamed he would not come home to her that evening. Instead, he would go home to his Father in Heaven.

That afternoon as his semi-load of logs was being unloaded, he went to check something beside the truck. Suddenly, a log slipped and crashed down on Ervin. It took his life; he lay still and dead. The angels carried him home to Heaven, for Heaven is the eternal home of all those who truly love the Lord.

Just because we love the Lord, that doesn't always protect us from accidents and sadness. But even when these things happen, God is with us.

The angels beckon me from heaven's open door,
And I can't feel at home in this world anymore.

—Albert E. Brumley, used by permission

Treasure Search

My times are in thy hand.

Psalm 31:15

READ LUKE 16:19–22

The Touch of the Angels

Lill sighed as she lay wearily on her pillow. Cancer was slowly but surely taking the life and strength from her body. Her mouth was dry, and her lips were cracked and parched. She was too weak, too tired, and too sick to do anything about it.

Each day, family and friends would lovingly try to meet her needs.

Lill was tempted to think, "Where is God, whom I have loved and served for so many years?"

Then one day she heard a gentle rushing in her room. To her surprise and delight, beside her bed was an angel in white. He lovingly and kindly touched her lips. They were so moist and refreshed. Then the angel was gone.

Later her sister breezed cheerily into the room, put some lip balm on her lips, fluffed her pillow, and brightened her day with loving words.

"Alta," Lill said, "Sometimes an angel comes and moistens my lips. It is always so refreshing. It lasts longer than when you or someone else puts lip balm on for me." Tears welled up in her eyes. "Truly, God has not left me alone."

God will not leave you alone; He sends His angels to comfort you.

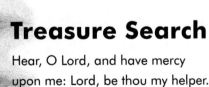

Treasure Search

Hear, O Lord, and have mercy
upon me: Lord, be thou my helper.

Psalm 30:10

READ PSALM 31:5, 15 AND PSALM 23:6

You Must Go Back

Lester was working hard picking tomatoes with his wife Betty in their little three-acre field. For several days he hadn't been well, and now he felt worse. "Betty," he sighed, "I can't pick one more tomato. I feel awfully sick and extremely tired."

The next morning, Lester's skin was a strange shade of yellow. They rushed him to the hospital. He was desperately ill with hepatitis.

The third day he was in the hospital, Lester was in critical condition. The doctors weren't sure he would make it. He had a great desire to go to heaven, even though he dearly loved his wife and their sweet baby.

That night while he slept, the Lord gave him a vision of heaven. He felt himself going home and was so glad and free. "Hallelujah! This is so wonderful," he thought. He looked back and saw his body lying on the hospital bed. Then he saw the pearly gates open wide and heard the sweetest, most wonderful singing. But a shining angel told him, "You must go back. You have a reason to live. There is so much work for you to do."

The next day, the doctor told him he looked wonderful. There was a sparkle in his eyes and a healthy color on his cheeks. Lester knew the Lord had sustained him. In a few weeks he was well and strong.

Today, thirty years later, Lester is a busy worker for the Lord. He holds many evangelistic meetings and is involved in missions. Numerous people come to him for counseling and help. He points them all to Jesus, the Great Physician, and helps them to find purpose and meaning in life.

God is preparing a heavenly home for all His children.

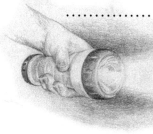

Treasure Search

For to me to live is Christ, and to die is gain. –Philippians 1:21

I awaked, for the Lord sustained me.

Psalm 3:5

READ PSALM 23

Angels and God's Fiery Chariots

The king of Syria was determined to capture the prophet Elisha, for Elisha would inform the king of Israel about the Syrian army's plans.

One morning Elisha's servant came running back to his master's house. He was shaking with fear. "Master, Master, what shall we do?" he cried. "This city is surrounded by fierce soldiers, horses, and chariots. They have come to catch you!"

Elisha calmly answered, "Don't be afraid; we have more help than they do." Then he bowed his head and prayed for his servant, "Lord, open his eyes that he may see."

God opened his eyes, and the servant saw that the surrounding mountains were full of God's horses and chariots of fire!

When the soldiers came near to catch Elisha, the prophet prayed that the Lord would blind them. God answered his prayer.

Elisha told the blind soldiers, "You are not in the right place. Follow me, and I will take you to the man you seek."

Elisha led the whole army to Samaria. There the king of Israel wanted to kill the Syrian army. "My father," he said to Elisha, "Shall I smite them? Shall I smite them?"

But Elisha said, "No. Give them bread to eat and water to drink and send them home to their master."

The king did as Elisha said and they never came into the land of Israel again.

(From 2 Kings 6:8–23)

With us is the Lord our God to help us!

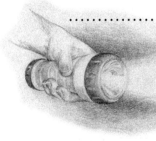

Treasure Search

The chariots of God are twenty thousand, even thousands of angels: the Lord is among them, as in Sinai, in the holy place. Psalm 68:17

READ 2 CHRONICLES 16:8, 9; 2 CHRONICLES 32:8, AND EXODUS 14:14

A Thrilling Escape

This poor man cried, and the Lord heard him, and saved him out of all his troubles. The angel of the Lord encampeth round about them that fear him, and delivereth them. O taste and see that the Lord is good: blessed is the man that trusteth in him. ~Psalm 34:6-8

Peter lay wrapped in sweet slumber, even though he was in prison and chained between two soldiers.

His friends were so sad that he was caught. They prayed every day that God would not let the evil King Herod kill Peter.

While Peter slept, suddenly an angel appeared and a light from heaven shone in that dark and dreary prison cell.

The angel shook Peter and told him to get up quickly. As he stood up, his chains fell off his hands.

The angel said, "Put on your coat and sandals and follow me."

Peter went with the angel. It seemed to him that he was only dreaming. As they came to the doors in the prison, each one opened. Even the last, huge iron gate just swung open. Peter passed through the open gate. He was free! He walked down the lonely deserted city street. The angel disappeared. Peter was now fully awake.

He said, "I know for sure that God sent His angel and saved me from wicked King Herod."

Peter went to the house of Mary where many of his friends were praying. Rhoda answered his knock. She heard Peter talk and was so excited she ran back in, but didn't open the door. "Peter is at the gate," she announced.

The others didn't believe it was Peter. He kept on knocking. They finally opened the door.

How they rejoiced together that the Lord brought him out of prison!

(From Acts 12:5–17)

Whate'er betide, beneath His wings of love abide, God will take care of you. —Civilla D. Martin

Treasure Search

And Moses said unto the people, Fear ye not, stand still, and see the salvation of the Lord, which he will shew to you to day: for the Egyptians whom ye have seen to day, ye shall see them again no more for ever.

The Lord shall fight for you and ye shall hold your peace.   Exodus 14:13, 14

READ PSALM 107:19 AND 2 SAMUEL 22:47

Prayer and Words

Pray all the time

A Praying Teacher and a Laughing Girl

Pray without ceasing. ~1 Thessalonians 5:17

Be careful for nothing; but in everything by prayer and supplication with thanksgiving let your requests be made known unto God. ~Philippians 4:6

What a lively and interesting bunch of students I had. Some of them had very black skin, others were brown Indians, and a few were "pale-faced" white. Each one was unique and special.

It was quite a job to keep all twenty of them happy and busy. There were some real mischief-makers in the bunch! Tommy could hardly hold still. Randy had a real stubborn streak. They kept me busy all day.

Most of the children walked home at 3:00. Then the peace and quiet was refreshing. It was a good time to pray. I loved to talk aloud to God, my best friend: "Lord, I feel weary tonight. You know how Jean disobeyed today. Then Joe pinched Tommy so hard he cried. I need your wisdom and help, Lord, to teach these dear children."

One evening when I was praying, suddenly Susie popped up from behind her desk. I hadn't seen her sneak back into the schoolroom. She was laughing and asked, "Teacher, who were you talking to?" She thought I had been talking to myself. Even when I told her I was praying, she still smiled, laughed, and ran out the door to tell her brother who was playing out by the sandy road with his homemade truck.

Pray about everything,
Pray every day, talk to God,
He is your friend,
And He loves you.

Treasure Search

Evening, and morning, and at noon, will I pray, and cry aloud: and he shall hear my voice.

Psalm 55:17

READ 2 THESSALONIANS 1:11

Should We Pray?

*And there arose another generation after them,
which knew not the Lord, nor yet the works
which he had done for Israel. —Judges 2:10*

The young man stomped out of his home. He was tired of going to church, tired of praying, tired of doing what Dad and Mom told him to do.

He decided, "I will live my own life!" So he moved far away to Florida. Now he could have his fun and sleep in late on Sunday if he wished and not bother with Dad and Mom's ideas.

Later, he married a woman who was not a Christian. They had a baby boy named Tom.

After many years had passed, they came back to Ohio to visit relatives. At his grandfather's house they all bowed their heads before they ate except Tom.

"Why are they bowing their heads?" he wondered. "These people sure have a different lifestyle."

When you are grown . . .

will you pray before you eat?

will you love the Lord?

will your children love to pray too?

We are only a generation away from heathendom.

Treasure Search

And these words, which I command thee this day, shall be in thine heart. And thou shalt teach them diligently unto thy children, and shalt talk of them when thou sittest in thine house, and when thou walkest by the way, and when thou liest down, and when thou risest up.

Deuteronomy 6:6, 7

READ DANIEL 6:10, 11

Saved From a Snake

God is our refuge and strength; a very present help in trouble. ~Psalm 46:1

For he shall give his angels charge over thee, to keep thee in all thy ways. ~Psalm 91:11

The fierce rays of the hot Belizean sun beat down on Mark as he bent and cut off a bunch of rice. He was with a native friend way back in a little field near the jungle. This was a small rice plantation, where all the work was done by hand, as it had been for hundreds of years. No tractor or truck could reach this rice field.

Mark was a missionary schoolteacher. Working in the great outdoors on Saturday was a nice diversion from teaching school.

Suddenly, he was gripped with fear, for very near him on the water was a large poisonous snake.

Quickly he called the native man. He came with his big sharp machete, but the snake had silently slithered away.

Gratefully, Mark thanked God for protecting his life. His mother was praying for him that day. Though she was thousands of miles away, God heard and answered. After all, distance is nothing to God.

Pray when you are happy.
Pray when you are scared.
Pray that God would protect you.

Treasure Search

The Lord is far from the wicked: but he heareth the prayer of the righteous.

Proverbs 15:29

READ PSALM 32:7 AND PSALM 46:7

Words

*Then shall ye call upon me, and ye shall go
and pray unto me, and I will hearken unto you.*

*And ye shall seek me, and find me, when ye
shall search for me with all your heart.*

~Jeremiah 29:12, 13

Words are powerful. The words that you speak have power to make others happy, glad, or sad.

A speaker once said, "There are seven words that would change the world. Only seven words! They are found in James 4:2. "Ye have not because ye ask not." If we want God's help and power we need to ask. Great things happen when we pray. All men of great spiritual influence have been strong men of prayer. Successful missionaries know how to meet God in prayer and have many prayer supporters.

Hannah prayed for a son and God gave her Samuel. Solomon prayed for wisdom and God made him the wisest of men. Paul and Silas prayed and God sent an earthquake.

Fathers and mothers need to pray every day for wisdom. They need God's help to have a happy, godly home.

Jesus prayed in the garden. He had strength, love, and courage to die on the cross. Because He died and rose again, we look forward to a heavenly home.

Do you pray and love to talk with God? Ask Him to lead and guide you each day.

God doesn't have any dumb children.
His children love to pray.

Treasure Search

Let the words of my mouth, and the meditation of my heart, be acceptable in thy sight, O Lord, my strength, and my redeemer.

Psalm 19:14

READ PSALM 55:17, EPHESIANS 4:29 AND PROVERBS 12:25

The Last Night

Pride goeth before destruction, and a haughty spirit before a fall. ~Proverbs 16:18

How shall we escape, if we neglect so great salvation; which at the first began to be spoken by the Lord, and was confirmed unto us by them that heard him. ~Hebrews 2:3

It was April 1912, when the huge, new, shiny ship, the Titanic, glided smoothly across the blue waters on its maiden voyage to New York.

The Titanic was the largest, most glamorous ship in all the world. It was as high as an eleven-story building and nearly as long as four city blocks. It had left England with a big show. There were two thousand, two hundred people on board. Many of them were very, very rich.

The Titanic was believed to be the safest ship afloat. Experts considered it to be unsinkable. When they were loading, a lady asked a deckhand, "Is this ship unsinkable?" He responded, "God Himself could not sink this ship!"

On the fifth day of the voyage, Captain Smith received six messages or warnings about dangerous icebergs. A nearby ship, the California, had radioed with a warning. The response from the Titanic's tired operator was, "Shut up, shut up, I'm busy!" That is, in part, why the California later did not respond when the Titanic tried to radio for help.

At 11:40 that night, the Titanic struck a huge iceberg, which ripped a three–hundred foot gash in its hull. Only two and one–half hours later, the Titanic sank. One thousand, five hundred of the people on board died. It was their last night. The ocean was their grave. What a tragedy!

Each one of us is on a voyage of life. If our trust is in ourselves or in our riches, our boat will sink. Only as we love the Lord and heed His Word can we be guided safely home to heaven.

We are safe when God is the captain of our ship.

Treasure Search

But he that shall endure unto the end,
the same shall be saved.

Matthew 24:13

READ PROVERBS 11:4 AND PSALM 20:7

Strong Words

*Set a watch, O Lord, before my mouth;
keep the door of my lips. —Psalm 141:3*

*Boast not thyself of tomorrow; for thou knowest not
what a day may bring forth. —Proverbs 27:1*

Huge highway bridges had fallen on their sides, homes were destroyed and buildings ruined in an earthquake that shook San Francisco, California, on October 17, 1989.

Engineers from Japan were soon on the scenes of ruin in California. They wanted to learn from the devastation what they could do to survive an earthquake in Japan.

Japanese building codes are strict; in fact, the strictest in the world. The engineers thought their buildings and highways would withstand an earthquake like the one that struck San Francisco. One Japanese engineer declared, "Our freeways would not have fallen!"

But in January 1995, a terrible earthquake shook parts of Japan. The poor city of Kobe suffered terrible devastation.

The main east-west highway fell over on its side. Its concrete pylons were snapped at their base, tipping one-half mile of four-lane highway on the street below. Cars and trucks lay smashed and crumbled. Many buildings and homes were in complete ruin. From this tragedy, Japanese engineers learned that they didn't know nearly as much about protection from earthquakes as they thought they did.

Each one of us needs to be careful about the words we use. Watch out for the words never and always. They are often not used honestly. "I would never do that." "You always act rude." "Why do you never play with me?" "She can always choose first."

With God's help your tongue can be honest and kind.

Treasure Search

Whereas ye know not what shall be on the morrow. For what is your life? It is even a vapour, that appeareth for a little time, and then vanisheth away.

For that ye ought to say, If the Lord will, we shall live, and do this, or that.

James 4:14, 15

READ JAMES 4:13–17

Courage

Have courage for the great sorrows of life.

And patience for the small ones.

And when you have accomplished your daily tasks

Go to sleep in peace. God is awake.

~Victor Hugo, Les Miserables

Courage

Wait on the Lord: be of good courage, and he shall strengthen thine heart: wait, I say, on the Lord. —Psalm 27:14

Courage is facing difficulty, danger, and pain with firmness, without fear.

It is:

- —bravery;
- —doing what is right no matter what happens, like the three Hebrew children who were thrown into the fiery furnace;
- —knowing God will help you;
- —fearless in the face of danger, like David when he faced Goliath.

Many years ago, when I was a young girl at home, we made a plaque entitled "Have courage." I hung it on my bedroom wall.

Have courage for the great sorrows of life
And patience for the small ones.
And when you have accomplished your daily tasks,
Go to sleep in peace.
God is awake.

—Victor Hugo, Les Miserables

Today, years later, I still remember it and can recite it.

It is important to memorize and learn good things when we are children!

Be courageous for Jesus!

Treasure Search

Be of good courage, and let us behave ourselves valiantly for our people, and for the cities of our God: and let the Lord do that which is good in his sight.

1 Chronicles 19:13

READ 1 CHRONICLES 22:13 AND DEUTERONOMY 31:6

People of Great Courage

Arise; for this matter belongeth unto thee: we also will be with thee: be of good courage, and do it. ~Ezra 10:4

The Bible is full of wonderful stories of men and women who had courage to do what is right.

Noah had courage to build a huge ark when no water was in sight. His courage saved his family.

Abraham had courage to obey when God said, "Offer up your only son, Isaac, whom you love." How could that make sense? Yet Abraham obeyed! Just as Abraham had the knife ready to slay Isaac, an angel called him out of Heaven. "Don't do it. Now I know you truly love the Lord. You were willing to give your all, your best."

Hannah had courage to give her young son Samuel in service for the Lord. Though Hannah probably missed her son very much, still she was willing to let Samuel work for Eli in the temple.

David faced that great giant Goliath. Knowing that God would help him gave David courage. David felled the giant with one small smooth stone.

Prayer and fasting gave Queen Esther courage to ask the king to save her people, the Jews. God saved the Jews from Haman's plot.

Daniel had courage to keep on praying to God after the king said, "Everyone must pray to me, or be thrown into the lions' den!" God saved Daniel even in the lions' den.

Heaven will be full of people who had courage to do what was right, no matter what it cost.

Knowing God gives you courage.

Treasure Search

And David said to Solomon his son, Be strong and of good courage, and do it: fear not, nor be dismayed: for the Lord God, even my God, will be with thee; he will not fail thee, nor forsake thee, until thou hast finished all the work for the service of the house of the Lord.　—1 Chronicles 28:20

READ PSALM 31:24

The Courageous Cat

Ye are of God, little children, and have overcome them: because greater is he that is in you, than he that is in the world. ~1 John 4:4

One morning as I looked out the window, I saw a funny little scene that reminded me of courage.

Fluffy, our orange and white cat, was on the alert because our neighbor's friendly brown beagle dog had stopped by for a visit. He was looking at the cat and yelping short little barks.

Fluffy arched her back and her hair stood on end. I expected her to turn and run up a nearby tree, but instead, this feisty little cat ran after the beagle. That dog turned tail and ran!

Presently, they stopped the chase. Maybe both cat and dog were surprised about such behavior, but after a bit, Fluffy chased the dog again, as if to say, "You go home, I live here!"

Our enemy, Satan, walks about as a roaring lion searching for someone to catch and devour. Alone, we are no match for the devil or lions. However, our God is all-powerful. When we cry to Jesus for help, Satan must flee.

God gives us courage to face each day.

Treasure Search

And Joshua said unto them, Fear not, nor be dismayed, be strong and of good courage: for thus shall the Lord do to all your enemies against whom ye fight.

Joshua 10:25

READ EPHESIANS 6:10 AND 2 CHRONICLES 32:7, 8

Kidnapped
Tan's Tale Part One

Only be thou strong and very courageous, that thou mayest observe to do according to all the law, which Moses my servant commanded thee: . . . Have not I commanded thee? Be strong and of a good courage; be not afraid, neither be thou dismayed: for the Lord thy God is with thee whithersoever thou goest. ~Joshua 1:7, 9

Nearly one hundred years ago in England, a little five-year-old boy, Stanley Clarke (Tan for short), was stolen by gypsies. It was a lovely autumn afternoon. Tan was on a walk with his big sister. She decided to stop and read while he ran ahead to meet his other sister, Jesse, coming home from school. Before Tan found Jesse, he saw an organ man with a monkey. Tan followed him, got lost in town, and then wandered into a gypsy camp.

The gypsies decided it would be profitable to keep such a cute, golden-haired boy. Tan was tired. After they gave him food, he soon fell asleep.

His family searched and searched for him that night and the next day. They were heartbroken to find no trace of the child they dearly loved.

In the morning, Tan wanted to go home. The gypsies kept promising he'd soon be there. At first, Tan thought it was exciting to ride in the gypsies' van pulled by horses. Also, he loved to play with a kitten they found for him.

Tan's godly mother had taught him to pray every morning and evening from the time he could say a few words; so each morning and night he would kneel in the gypsy van to pray. The gypsies tried to get Tan to stop, but nothing could shake him from speaking to God (as Tan called it).

Hardly a day passed that the gypsy family did not lie, steal food from gardens, or deceive in some way. They told Tan his own mother had died. Tan sobbed and sobbed. He thought it was true, yet Tan had courage to keep on praying.

God cares and sees each tear drop fall.

Treasure Search

God is our refuge and strength, a very present help in trouble.

Psalm 46:1

READ ISAIAH 44:8

I Will not Steal
Tan's Tale Part Two

He will turn again, he will have compassion upon us; he will subdue our iniquities; and thou wilt cast all their sins into the depths of the sea. —Micah 7:19

Then Peter and the other apostles answered and said, We ought to obey God rather than men. —Acts 5:29

The first year Tan was with the gypsies, he was, for the most part, treated kindly. This was largely due to Jack, a rough gypsy lad who took a liking to the little chap.

At times, Tan was ordered to steal from some garden or haystack. He always firmly refused. This greatly angered Mr. Smith (the gypsy father), but Jack always shielded and protected Tan. Many times when Tan knelt to pray, Mr. Smith would mock him, but Tan would not stop praying. He knew it was right! Prayer was instilled in his tender, young heart by his godly mother.

One morning Jack took Tan on a walk to the seaside. Tan just stood and gazed at the sea. Jack asked, "What are yer thinking?"

Tan in his sweet voice replied, "I was thinking about where God puts the sins of people who trust Him."

"What der yer mean?" asked Jack.

"My sister taught me that verse," said Tan. "'Thou wilt cast all my sins into the depths of the sea.' Do you think He will cast your sins in there, Jack?"

Tan's prayers, and the words he spoke, were showing the rough gypsy lad the way to God.

Resolve to always do what is right.

Treasure Search

The Lord is my light and my salvation; whom shall I fear? the Lord is the strength of my life; of whom shall I be afraid?

Psalm 27:1

READ PSALM 55:17

Longing for Mother

Tan's Tale Part Three

Are not five sparrows sold for two farthings, and not one of them is forgotten before God? But even the very hairs of your head are all numbered. Fear not therefore: ye are of more value than many sparrows. —Luke 12:6, 7

Tan had been with the gypsies nearly a year. Memories of home were growing dim.

One evening a group of laughing men walked by the gypsies' camp. One of them accidentally dropped a gold coin in the dust. Tan's sharp eyes noticed, as did Mr. Smith's. He told Tan, "Go, get it for me, sharp now! Don't let the gents see you." Tan ran, picked up the coveted piece of gold and ran after the man, saying, "You dropped your money." The man was delighted at the honest gypsy chap and rewarded him with a six-pence.

Tan ran back with a smile, but that quickly faded when he saw how angry Mr. Smith was. He shouted, "I'll teach you not to disobey." He brought a stick down hard over Tan's shoulders. He was ready to strike again when Jack darted forward. This made Mr. Smith furious. He hit his son across the face with an old whip and told him to get out! Jack left in a rage.

Tan wept and wept that Jack, his only friend, was gone. His life became difficult.

One day he was whipped because he refused to steal potatoes. Some days were so wearisome, he often wished he could die and go to his mother in heaven. He thought he had no real family who loved him.

Yet his heavenly Father had not forgotten or forsaken him.

God understands.

Treasure Search

Blessed are ye, when men shall revile you, and persecute you, and shall say all manner of evil against you falsely, for my sake. Rejoice, and be exceeding glad: for great is your reward in heaven: for so persecuted they the prophets which were before you.   Matthew 5:11, 12

READ MATTHEW 10:29, 31

Home at Last
Tan's Tale Part Four

Men ought always to pray, and not to faint. ~Luke 18:1
I will instruct thee and teach thee in the way which thou shalt go: I will guide thee with mine eye. ~Psalm 32:8

One moonlit night, Tan ran away. He thought he must go to find Jack!

He was not afraid as he ran and walked along the lonely road to town. At early dawn, he was so faint and tired that he sank down by the roadside and was soon fast asleep. Angels kept watch over his stony pillow.

Some kind boys found him on their way to school. One even gave him jam sandwiches. Tan knelt by the dusty road and thanked the Lord, who even now was guiding him by the right way.

During the night, unknown to Tan, he had passed the house where his family lived. Only recently, they had moved to the country. Every day they still prayed that God would send their treasure home if he was still on the earth.

Tan spent a lonely day in town. That night a policeman found him sitting on a doorstep, crying, forlorn, and alone. The big man spoke kindly to Tan and took him to the police station for the night.

The next day Tan's sister saw a notice in the paper. "Found: a little boy, approximately eight, ran away from gypsies. Cannot recall his past, but affirms he has not always been with them. Only known name—Tan."

His sister prayed, "Oh God, help me find him." Hurriedly she hitched up their pony to the cart and headed for town. Quickly she rushed to the police station. At first glance she wasn't sure this was her brother, but soon she found a scar he had gotten as a toddler. Tan was found! "Praise God!" she said, as she clasped an astonished Tan to her.

Oh, how the family rejoiced that night! God had heard their cries and prayers. Tan was safely home.

How wonderful that God hears and answers prayer!

Treasure Search

What time I am afraid, I will trust in thee.

Psalm 56:3

READ ISAIAH 12:2, 3

My Wonderful Treasure

I have a wonderful treasure,
The gift of God without measure,
And so we travel together,
My Bible and I!

—Harry Dixon Loes

Do you love the Bible? Here are some things that show evidence of a love for God's word.

1. Pay attention in family worship. Read the Bible loud and clear.

2. Do your Sunday School lesson cheerfully.

3. Memorize your Bible memory verse.

4. Teach younger brothers and sisters Bible verses.

5. Listen to what the preacher says in church.

And that from a child thou hast known the holy scriptures, which are able to make thee wise unto salvation through faith which is in Christ Jesus. —2 Timothy 3:15

My watchword in life's battle,
My chart on life's dark sea,
The precious Holy Bible
Shall ere' my teacher be.

Love for God's word enables you to be strong for Jesus.

Treasure Search

Let us hear the conclusion of the whole matter: Fear God, and keep his commandments: for this is the whole duty of man.

Ecclesiastes 12:13

READ PSALM 119:9, 105, 127

Know Your Treasure

Ever learning, and never able to come to the knowledge of the truth. ~2 Timothy 3:7

In her kitchen, my mother had a picture of fruit with "Love, Joy, Peace" written on it and a caption which read, "The Fruit of the Spirit."

A young man was visiting in her home. Jim was tall, with dark wavy hair, well-dressed, smart, and mannerly. He had just graduated from a prestigious college. He saw the picture of fruit and wondered, "What does that mean?" He had never heard of the fruit of the Spirit. Mom told him, "Jim, those words are from Scripture. People who love God have the wonderful fruit of love, joy, and peace in their lives."

In all Jim's many years of going to school, through everything he learned, he had missed what is most important—the Word of God.

When people come into your home, is there visible evidence that you love Jesus? Bible verses and mottos on the wall are a witness to draw others and ourselves to the Lord.

Can men tell that you love Jesus?

Treasure Search

Study to shew thyself approved unto God, a workman that needeth not to be ashamed, rightly dividing the word of truth.

2 Timothy 2:15

READ PROVERBS 1:7 AND PROVERBS 2:6

God's Powerful Word

For the word of God is quick, and powerful, and sharper than any two-edged sword, piercing even to the dividing asunder of soul and spirit, and of the joints and marrow, and is a discerner of the thoughts and intents of the heart.
~Hebrews 4:12

During World War I, a young man was traveling by train, his suitcase sitting on the floor beside his seat. On the suitcase were the words, "You can't run with the world and walk with God."

Across the aisle sat an older man. He noticed the message on the young man's suitcase. His eyes just seemed to be drawn to it. Finally, he said to the young man, "I wish you would turn your suitcase around."

The young man promptly turned his suitcase around, and on the other side was a message also. "Except ye repent, ye shall all likewise perish" (Luke 13:3).

The older man took one look, turned away, and ignored the young man and his suitcase for the rest of the trip.

What do you do with the Word of God? Do you love it and try to obey it? Or does its message convict you of wrong, and so you just turn away from the Bible?

The happiest people are those who truly love God's Word.

Treasure Search

And now, Lord, behold their threatenings: and grant unto thy servants, that with all boldness they may speak thy word.

Acts 4:29

READ JAMES 1:22 AND ROMANS 1:16

Burning the Bible

Heaven and earth shall pass away, but my words shall not pass away. ~Matthew 24:35

But the word of the Lord endureth for ever. And this is the word which by the gospel is preached unto you. ~1 Peter 1:25

Many of the children of Israel had forgotten about God. They loved idols and lived wickedly. God, in His love and mercy, sent them a warning through Jeremiah the prophet. They had a chance to hear God and turn from their wicked ways to God their Father. Jeremiah's helper Baruch wrote the message on a scroll.

The king's princes heard the message and were afraid. They decided that King Jehoiakim must be told, but first they told Jeremiah and Baruch to hide.

A fire was crackling merrily on the hearth in the king's winter house. Its warmth dispelled the chilling cold, yet all was not merry in the room. The king sat with an angry scowl on his face. One of his men was reading God's message of judgment and destruction. King Jehoiakim was so upset and angry, he didn't wait to hear it all. Piece by piece he cut off the writings with his penknife and threw them into the fire.

Three of his princes had courage and begged him, "Don't burn words from God!" But he gave no heed and stubbornly went on cutting and burning till there were none left!

Sure enough, he wanted Jeremiah and Baruch arrested, but the Lord hid them. Then God told Jeremiah to write the same words again, plus many more.

(Taken from Jeremiah 36)

Burning God's Word does not destroy its power.

Treasure Search

For the Lord is good; his mercy is everlasting; and his truth endureth to all generations.

Psalm 100:5

READ DEUTERONOMY 30:15, 16 AND PSALM 119:89

It Would Not Burn!

*Casting all your care upon him;
for he careth for you.* ~1 Peter 5:7

There were big piles of dirty laundry in the house. Betty and her husband had just gotten back from a week of mission work in New York City. Now she had a lot of work to do at home.

"Why don't I run to town with all the dirty wash? I'll just stick it all in the washers and soon be done," she mused.

Before long she was on her way. While driving along, she was talking to God, thanking Him for His love and goodness, praising Him for their happy home, and praying for God's wisdom and strength for her day.

A while later, she was happy to be going home with all the laundry clean and folded in neat stacks. She was nearly home when suddenly she saw many cars and trucks in their driveway. What could be going on? "My children," she thought. "My children! Did something happen to them at school?"

But then she saw smoke and fire billowing from their house. "Oh, how can this be?" She jumped out of the car. Her husband came running. Betty fell crying into his arms. "It's okay, dear," he comforted her. "We're all here and safe."

The next day, when everything was no longer smoldering, they walked through the remains of what had been their home. What a sight! All the walls were smoked and black, and the furniture was charred ruins. Betty looked into their bedroom for one last time. She stopped short in surprise. There on the black smoky wall was a plaque that had not burned. The motto leaped out at her: "He Cares for You." What a tender reminder of God's love and care amid all the black rubble and ruins of their house!

No matter what happens, remember, God does care.

Treasure Search

For his anger endureth but a moment; in his favour is life: weeping may endure for a night, but joy cometh in the morning.

Psalm 30:5

READ PSALM 27:13, 14

The Greatest Flood Ever

The earth also was corrupt before God, and the earth was filled with violence. . . . And God said unto Noah, "The end of all flesh is come before me; for the earth is filled with violence through them; and, behold, I will destroy them with the earth. ~Genesis 6:11, 13

And every living substance was destroyed which was upon the face of the ground, both man, and cattle, and the creeping things, and the fowl of the heaven; and they were destroyed from the earth: and Noah only remained alive, and they that were with him in the ark. ~Genesis 7:23

The Bible is a very important part of everyday life in the Christian home. Babies hear their parents read the Bible. Soon they enjoy Bible story pictures. Before long they love Bible stories and learn simple verses.

What a blessing this is!

A preacher worked at a sawmill. He was talking about the Bible with his friend Marion. They were discussing the terrible flood in the days of Noah. A young man was listening. He had never heard the story before.

"Where was this flood?" he asked. "How many people drowned? You mean it actually covered the highest mountains on the earth?" He could hardly believe it! But yes, every high mountain peak was covered. The whole earth was flooded. All mankind except Noah and his family were drowned.

How unfortunate that even in the United States where there are many Bibles and many churches, there are people who grow up not being taught the Word of God.

Share the good news of Jesus today!

Treasure Search

For he established a testimony in Jacob, and appointed a law in Israel, which he commanded our fathers, that they should make them known to their children: That the generation to come might know them, even the children which should be born; who should arise and declare them to their children: That they might set their hope in God, and not forget the works of God, but keep his commandments.   Psalm 78:5–7

READ DEUTERONOMY 6:6, 7 AND 2 TIMOTHY 3:15

New York City Boy

But ye shall receive power, after that the Holy Ghost is come upon you: and ye shall be witnesses unto me both in Jerusalem, and in all Judaea, and in Samaria, and unto the uttermost part of the earth. —Acts 1:8

So shall my word be that goeth forth out of my mouth: it shall not return unto me void, but it shall accomplish that which I please, and it shall prosper in the thing whereto I sent it. —Isaiah 55:11

Every summer for a number of years, a black boy from New York City spent a few weeks with our farm family. He came through the Fresh Air Program, which gave city children the chance to enjoy country living.

Roshan was a mannerly and pleasant young lad. Our rambling, old farmhouse with no TV must have been strange to him. He didn't lack for entertainment though. Three energetic farmer boys kept him busy. There were ponies to ride, cows to milk, eggs to gather, hogs to feed, and dogs and cats to play with.

Roshan enjoyed reading. We gave him some Bible story books. One morning he said he was reading about Adam and Eve (he had never heard the story). He was amazed that God made them out of dust! The story of Noah and the flood fascinated him. He also enjoyed our summer Bible school.

With the passing of years we lost contact with Roshan. Only God knows, but maybe Roshan's life was touched by God on a farm long ago.

Touch a life for Jesus.

Treasure Search

And he said unto them, Go ye into all the world, and preach the gospel to every creature.

Mark 16:15

READ ACTS 22:15

Do It
for the Lord!

This poem is put here to fan flames of commitment in the minds of children. Parents can be channels through whom their children begin ministering to others.

Do you take time to lend a hand
    When someone is in dire need?
Or are you so busy with your own
    That you don't care or give heed?

Do you take time, do you care
    When a friend is sick or dying?
Do you go minister comfort and hope
    And empathize with their tears and crying?

Do you take time for a little child,
    Read, play, and listen to his woes?
Will he grow up to be a helpful man
    Because you had time for his heart throes?

Do you take time for the aged man
　　When he comes to your house to sit and chat?
He lives alone and is often lonely.
　　You can put out a welcome mat.

Do you take time to go to a mission
　　To sing and talk to dismal men?
They need to see God's love and kindness.
　　Will you take time to be a friend?

Do you want to sit and talk
　　When someone needs a friend to share?
Or must you keep at work and duties,
　　Where are the people who really care?

Do you take time to go to prison
　　And bring good news to wretched souls?
Pointing the lost to Jesus Christ
　　Is an important heavenly goal.

O, you'd have time if Jesus came,
　　Yet, He does come and He is here!
For ministering to those in need,
　　Is doing it for the Lord we love so dear.

Treasure Search

And the King shall answer and say unto them, Verily I say unto you, Inasmuch as ye have done it unto one of the least of these my brethren, ye have done it unto me.

Matthew 25:40

READ MARK 9:41 AND HEBREWS 6:10

Thirsty and Ye Gave Me Drink

Cast me not off in the time of old age; forsake me not when my strength faileth. ~Psalm 71:9

Hearken unto thy father that begat thee, and despise not thy mother when she is old. ~Proverbs 23:22

Some people are so thirsty for love; will you love them?

The nursing home did not have nearly as many people in it as usual, for many of the guests were invited home to their families on Christmas Day. Some were left behind though: those who had no living relatives or caring friends nearby. Those whose children didn't want to be bothered with Grandma and Grandpa on Christmas Day.

Into this nursing home came a happy family of four small children with their parents, Joe and Jane. It was Christmas morning. They were overflowing with cheer and gladness. Little old ladies beamed with happiness as the children came to their rooms singing O Come, Little Children, Away In a Manger, and Silent Night.

One sweet old lady in a wheelchair followed the family from room to room. She loved holding the smaller children and giving them wheelchair rides.

Jane asked a small white-haired lady about her family. She replied, "I have none. I was an old maid and taught school for thirty-six years." This lady loved having someone to talk to and showed them a picture of her relatives.

When Jane and Joe and the children left, the lady in the wheelchair followed them right to the door!

Treasure Search

Pure religion and undefiled before God and the Father is this, To visit the fatherless and widows in their affliction, and to keep himself unspotted from the world.

James 1:27

READ LUKE 6:31 AND MATTHEW 7:12

Naked and Ye Clothed Me

*Now there was at Joppa a certain
disciple named Tabitha, which by interpretation
is called Dorcas: this woman was full of good
works and almsdeeds which she did.* ~Acts 9:36

Dorcas lived long ago. The Bible says she was full of good works. Dorcas helped poor widows. She sewed coats and other clothes for them. Suddenly one day, she became sick. Her friends tried their best to care for her, but she died. Two men quickly went to get Peter, their preacher. He came to the house where Dorcas lay in death's peaceful repose.

The widows Dorcas had helped were there, weeping and showing Peter the coats Dorcas had made for them.

Peter sent them all out of the room, knelt in prayer, and then said, "Dorcas, arise!"

God's power brought Dorcas back to life again! How her friends rejoiced! Many people heard of this miracle and believed in God.

(Story from Acts 9.)

Dorcas was full of good works, not only good words.

Treasure Search

Favour is deceitful, and beauty is vain: but a woman that feareth the Lord, she shall be praised.

Proverbs 31:30

READ 1 TIMOTHY 5:10 AND TITUS 3:8

Hungry, and Ye Fed Me

But my God shall supply all your need according to his riches in glory by Christ Jesus.
–Philippians 4:19

In the cool freshness of the early morning, Nancy knelt by her bed to pray. She loved to commune with her Lord and Maker. Each morning she liked to pray, "Lord, what wilt thou have me do today?"

This morning Nancy felt burdened for her friend Jane. She was so poor, and her husband was sick. "Lord," Nancy prayed, "help them, meet their needs, give them courage to continue to live for you." Nancy paused for a few moments. She could hear parrots and other tropical birds squawking and singing. They were praising their Maker, too. Though she heard no audible voice, Nancy knew God was speaking, "I want you to help Jane. I will meet her needs through you."

Later Jane knocked on Nancy's door. Sad and discouraged, she leaned against the kitchen counter. Tears ran in little rivers down her black cheeks, "I don't know what we can do," she sobbed. "No food or money in our house. Doesn't God care about us?"

"Jane," said Nancy, "whatever comes for me in the mail tomorrow, the Lord wants me to give to you. I believe something will come!"

The next day Nancy went to town for groceries and supplies for the mission. They had quite a load. Nancy's heart sank when the driver said, "I won't bother to cross the bridge and get the mail today." She just kept quiet and trusted God to work things out.

Late that evening she heard a vehicle outside. Her friend Dorothy had come to spend the weekend and she had the mail. Eagerly Nancy reached for it. There was a big long white envelope for her. "Praise the Lord," she exclaimed. Excitedly she opened it and found a $100 check. Never before had she gotten such a large gift by mail. "Praise the Lord. Oh, praise the Lord!" she rejoiced.

Jane too was blessed and overwhelmed with the gift. Her faith in God was strengthened. He had supplied her every need.

The Lord will supply—His riches never run dry!

Treasure Search

But whoso hath this world's good, and seeth his brother have need, and shutteth up his bowels of compassion from him, how dwelleth the love of God in him?

1 John 3:17

READ MATTHEW 7:7, LUKE 18:1, AND LUKE 6:38

A Stranger, and Ye Took Me In

*For I was an hungred, and ye gave me meat:
I was thirsty, and ye gave me drink: I was a
stranger, and ye took me in. ~Matthew 25:35*

*Be not forgetful to entertain strangers: for thereby some
have entertained angels unawares. ~Hebrews 13:2*

A stranger is someone with whom you've had no personal acquaintance. A stranger may be a foreigner, or a person who is not a member of your family, group, or community.

What will you do with a stranger?

An old man from West Virginia was traveling through Ohio. He stopped at Maranatha Church for the evening prayer meeting. He was a stranger. After the service, some of the men met and talked with him. One of the men invited the old man along home for the night. The stranger stayed at their home and appreciated their kindness, good food, and a warm bed.

The ladies were busy quilting at the sewing circle. A visitor was there whom most had never met. Some went to welcome and talk with her, others just passed on by.

A new boy comes to school. Will you be one of those who will stop and ask him to join in a game or invite him to eat lunch with you?

It is easiest to just stick to your good old friends, but you can take time to be kind and friendly to strangers, talk to them, share your food, and take an interest in their lives.

Someday you may be a stranger. Will anyone take you in?

Reaching out to a stranger is showing kindness to Jesus. Christ is more among us than we think He is.

Treasure Search

Love ye therefore the stranger: for ye were strangers in the land of Egypt.

Deuteronomy 10:19

READ 3 JOHN 5

In Prison and Ye Came Unto Me

Remember them that are in bonds, as bound with them; and them which suffer adversity, as being yourselves also in the body. ~Hebrews 13:3

Elizabeth Fry stood at the door of the Newgate Women's Prison. The prison sounded and smelled awful! Women were hollering at each other and babies were crying.

"You don't want to go in there to that bunch of witches and animals," said the guard. But Elizabeth, a Quaker, did go. She wanted to share God's love and kindness. She talked to the women and read the Bible to them.

The prison was crowded, very dirty, and filthy. She persuaded the prison keeper to send in water, soap, brushes, and clean straw for bedding, then she helped the women clean up the prison.

There were children in prison with their mothers. She encouraged them to start a school for their children. She sent slates, reading books, and chalk for the prison school.

Sometimes she brought extra food. She got the women busy sewing quilts and other things.

Her love and kindness brightened so many days. Her prayer each morning was, "What can I do for Jesus today?" She was a mother of eleven children, yet she didn't complain of too much work, and she always made time to help others.

In early 1820, she helped establish a home for bad little neglected girls (ages 7–13) who had been caught stealing. She also established shelters for women when they came out of prison.

All this was for the sake of Christ. Her motto was, "Whate'er I do in anything, to do it as to thee!"

To whom can you show kindness?

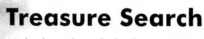

Treasure Search

Naked, and ye clothed me: I was sick, and ye visited me: I was in prison, and ye came unto me.
Matthew 25:36

READ PSALM 102:19, 20

Sick and Ye Visited Me

Naked, and ye clothed me: I was sick, and ye visited me: I was in prison, and ye came unto me. ~Matthew 25:36

Clara was sick due to a heart condition, which caused her health slowly to ebb away. It was difficult being unable to work and not having enough strength and energy to attend church regularly or to go away to visit friends.

Sometimes she got discouraged and wondered, Is my life of any use; what can I do for the Lord?

Clara grew weaker and thinner. She became so weak that she was confined to a hospital bed. She needed nursing around the clock. Her husband, Ura, and their children faithfully stayed with her, meeting her needs. They sat by her bed, held her hand, and sang and prayed.

Life often seemed dreary and monotonous. Thankfully, Clara

had many Christian friends who cared, visited, and did what they could to brighten her days. Through her suffering, her friends meant so much to her.

One evening some friends called. "Can we come over to visit and sing for Clara?"

"Yes, certainly, but only stay for fifteen minutes because Clara is so weak and ill."

Clara, looking weary, lay in her hospital bed. When four little children came in with their parents, her eyes brightened. She just watched those fresh, healthy, happy children's faces as they joyfully sang songs of Jesus and heaven.

It was only about ten days later that Clara was called home to heaven. Her tears and pain were forever gone. Perfect rest, joy, and peace are hers forevermore!

Do you take time to visit the sick?

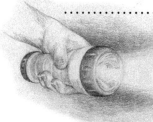

Treasure Search

I will seek that which was lost, and bring again that which was driven away, and will bind up that which was broken, and will strengthen that which was sick: but I will destroy the fat and the strong; I will feed them with judgment.

Ezekiel 34:16

READ GALATIANS 6:10

Contentment

In my Father's house are many mansions . . .

John 14:2

Contentment

How excellent is thy lovingkindness, O God!
Therefore the children of men put their trust under the shadow of thy wings. They shall be abundantly satisfied with the fatness of thy house; and thou shalt make them drink of the river of thy pleasures. ~Psalm 36:7, 8

Blessed is the man whom thou choosest, and causest to approach unto thee, that he may dwell in thy courts. ~Psalm 65:4

Contentment is:

—being happy with what you have
—counting your blessings, not just wishing for more
—an uncomplaining acceptance of one's life
—knowing God is in control

GET IT FOR ME!

A little girl, not quite two years old, was so comfortable on some soft cushions on the sofa. Happily, she turned the pages of a small colorful Bible story book. She was enjoying the pictures until she came to one with a little girl holding a lavender purse.

"Ugh, ugh, purse, purse, purse," she said, and with her little fingers she tried to grab the purse out of the book!

Her mother sat there watching, and wondered, "Am I that way, too? Quite content and happy till I look around and see what other people have? Why do I compare myself with those who have more than I do?"

Knowing and loving Jesus are the keys to true contentment.

Treasure Search

Blessed are all they that put their trust in him.

Psalm 2:12

READ PSALM 34:8

Satisfied With a Cottage

Let not your heart be troubled: ye believe in God, believe also in me. In my Father's house are many mansions: if it were not so, I would have told you. I go to prepare a place for you. ~John 14:1, 2

Here is a little story that gave Ira Forest Stanphill the inspiration for the song, "I'm Satisfied with Just a Cottage Below."

A rich man was traveling through a very poor part of the country. He came to a house so badly in need of paint and repairs that he wondered how it could still be standing. Most of the glass was broken out of the windows and replaced by oiled paper. Even parts of the roof were missing.

Playing out in front of this house, was a happy little boy of eight or nine. The rich man felt an urge to stop and talk with the boy. He loved children and felt sorry for the lad, so he stopped.

He told the little boy he was sorry he had to live in such poor surroundings. The little fellow replied, "Oh, mister, I won't have to live in this house forever. You see, mister, just over the hilltop up there my Dad has been building a house for Mother and us children. I don't know when it will be done, or when we will move in, but mister, I won't have to live here forever, no, siree!"

This little lad must've had a wonderful mother who was happy because she had Jesus! Happy even though she lived in a shabby house. They believed in Jesus, who is preparing a mansion in heaven for all His blessed children!

When we have Jesus we have the Best.
The fanciest house does not give happiness and rest.
Only Jesus gives true contentment.

Treasure Search

For he looked for a city which hath foundations, whose builder and maker is God.

Hebrews 11:10

READ HEBREWS 12:2

Blind and Happy

Let your conversation be without covetousness; and be content with such things as ye have: for he hath said, I will never leave thee, nor forsake thee. —Hebrews 13:5

A little girl was born on March 24, 1820. Her name was Fanny Crosby. How happy her parents must have been with this precious little baby girl! But alas, at six weeks of age, she caught a cold. Her eyes became red and inflamed. A well-meaning country doctor put hot mustard poultices on her eyes. The terrible result was blindness! Not long after that, Fanny's father died. When Fanny was five, kind neighbors collected enough money to send her to a famous eye doctor. After the doctor gently examined her, he said, "Poor little girl, she will always be blind."

Fanny's Grandmother was a wonderful lady who loved the Lord very much. She said, "I will be Fanny's eyes." She described gorgeous sunsets and sunrises to Fanny and told her that her great God painted them in the sky. She taught Fanny God's Word while they gently rocked on Grandma's rocking chair. First one verse, then more; later, chapters and entire books of the Bible. Fanny loved her godly grandmother very much. At the age of eight, Fanny was already a poet. She wrote:

O, what a happy soul I am!
Although I cannot see
I am resolved that in this world
Contented I will be.

How many blessings I enjoy
That other people don't;
To weep and sigh because I'm blind
I cannot and I won't.

Happiness is found when we "see" God.

Treasure Search

O satisfy us early with thy mercy;
that we may rejoice and be glad all our days.

Psalm 90:14

READ LUKE 16:19–22

A Sweet Singer

Not that I speak in respect of want: for I have learned, in whatsoever state I am, therewith to be content. ~Philippians 4:11

But godliness with contentment is great gain. For we brought nothing into this world, and it is certain we can carry nothing out. And having food and raiment let us be therewith content. ~1 Timothy 6:6-8

Fanny Crosby wrote between eight and nine thousand songs! More than anyone else ever did.

When she became a Christian, she was so filled with joy that she penned these words: Blessed assurance, Jesus is mine! Oh, what a foretaste of glory divine!

Fanny even thanked God for the privilege of being blind. She said blindness helped her write songs: she wasn't disturbed by things she saw. She did look forward to being able to see in heaven someday. A lot of her songs are about sight. One example is, Someday the silver cord will break and I shall see Him face to face.

Fanny was a woman of prayer. Before writing a hymn, she would kneel and ask God to help her. She was so blessed by God's answers to prayer that she wrote, All the way my Saviour leads me; What have I to ask beside?

Fanny cared about others. She would go to Bowery Mission in New York and talk with the poor men there. Once, after the service, an eighteen-year-old boy wanted to talk with her. "I have promised to meet my mother in heaven," he said. "But this is impossible because I am wicked and living for the devil." Fanny told him, "No sin is too hard for God to forgive. Why don't we pray together?" They knelt, and he confessed his sins and found God. "Now I can meet my mother in heaven," he said.

That night, Fanny penned the words of the soul-stirring hymn, Rescue the Perishing, Care for the Dying.

Fanny faithfully lived for Jesus till her death at the age of ninety-five. On her tombstone are the words, "She hath done what she could."

Are you doing what you can for Jesus?

Treasure Search

Thou wilt shew me the path of life:
in thy presence is fulness of joy; at thy
right hand there are pleasures for evermore.

Psalm 16:11

READ PSALM 17:15

A Happy Chick

Because thou hast been my help, therefore in the shadow of thy wings will I rejoice. ~Psalm 63:7

How excellent is thy lovingkindness, O God! therefore the children of men put their trust under the shadow of thy wings. ~Psalm 36:7

One evening I went out to the barn. A delightful sight met my eyes. A small bantam hen was resting on the hay. Peeping from under her wings was a cute little chick with bright beady eyes. He looked so perfectly satisfied, cozy, secure, safe, and warm under his mother's wings. He was warm, protected, and content all through the night.

CLOSE TO DADDY

Night was falling and a little boy was walking with his daddy through a woods, over a narrow path that led to home. "Daddy," said the little boy, "hold my hand; I am a little scared." His daddy held his little hand and on they went. After a while the shadows in the woods looked darker and more scary. Something big seemed to be moving behind a tall tree. "Daddy," said the boy again. "Daddy, please hold me; I am scared, and if I am in your arms I feel safe and happy." The kind strong man bent down and picked up his little boy, who nestled snugly against his daddy's chest. They were soon safely home.

CLOSE TO JESUS

God loves you and wants you to keep close to Him. Just like a chick who is with its mother, or a little boy with his daddy, we are safe with Jesus through life's dangers and troubles.

How do we keep close to Jesus? Jesus says, "Come to Me." We come and keep close when we love Jesus, talk to Him, and love what He tells us in the Bible.

Picture yourself
"Safe in the Arms of Jesus."

Treasure Search

He shall cover thee with his feathers, and under his wings shalt thou trust: his truth shall be thy shield and buckler.

Psalm 91:4

READ MATTHEW 23:37

I Want a Bike

Hell and destruction are never full; so the eyes of man are never satisfied. ~Proverbs 27:20

He that loveth silver shall not be satisfied with silver; nor he that loveth abundance with increase; this is also vanity. ~Ecclesiastes 5:10

Lester was very happy. He had just gotten what he wanted for his twelfth birthday—a bike! It had shiny chrome fenders even though it was a used bike.

"It sure will be nice to ride my bike to school now instead of walking, and I'll be able to get around town fast!" he rejoiced.

The first morning Lester rode his bike to school, he parked it out front. All his friends could see he finally had a bike!

Lester was so happy with that bike and enjoyed riding it every day, until something happened. His bike still worked fine, but one of his friends came to school with a shiny, new three-speed bike. That day, Lester parked his bike behind the school.

That evening Lester said, "Dad, do you think you could get a three-speed bike for me? They pedal much easier and I could get around faster too."

But alas, Dad said, "No. Yours is a good strong bike. Learn to be satisfied with what you have."

Dad's words were true. That bike lasted many years. Lester learned that to keep up with his friends was not what made him happy.

Make up your mind to be content.
Enjoy the things you have!

Treasure Search

Wherefore do ye spend money for that which is not bread? and your labor for that which satisfieth not? hearken diligently unto me, and eat ye that which is good, and let your soul delight itself in fatness.

Isaiah 55:2

READ ROMANS 12:15

Oh, to Be Tall

And they were beyond measure astonished, saying, He hath done all things well. ~Mark 7:37

Yet the Lord will command his lovingkindness in the day-time, and in the night his song shall be with me, and my prayer unto the God of my life. ~Psalm 42:8

"Oh Mom, why am I so short?" Twila wailed as she ran into the house, "Doris always beats me in races. It's not fair, her legs are much longer!"

"God made us all different, dear," replied her mother. "The Bible says, 'God hath done all things well.' Some people just don't grow tall. Accept yourself as God made you. There are many things you can do!" Twila was comforted and ran out to play.

She never thought too much about it until she was older. She realized she was a dwarf, and different from girls her age. "My fingers are so short and stubby," Twila sighed. "Oh, I wish they were long and slender. I wish I had more hair, too!"

"He loves me, He made me, and I will accept myself as I am. Why should I go through life annoyed because of things I cannot control? It would be so nice and comforting if there were another dwarf my age nearby so we could really identify with each other. At least I do have many friends. Best of all—I have Jesus," she mused. "That is such a joy and contentment. God made me to honor and glorify Him. What a comfort it is, that when things really bother me, I can go to God in prayer."

Twila often seems happier than girls who are normal-sized. It is because she knows what is most important: a heart submitted to God. She is a lovely young lady with a smile on her face.

Key to happiness—
Accepting things you cannot change.

Treasure Search

Nay but, O man, who art thou that repliest against God? Shall the thing formed say to him that formed it, Why hast thou made me thus?

Romans 9:20

READ PSALM 139:13–16 AND ISAIAH 43:7

The Crippled Girl

And we know that all things work together for good to them that love God, to them who are the called according to his purpose. ~Romans 8:28

Not slothful in business; fervent in spirit; serving the Lord. ~Romans 12:11

"Hello, is Ellen there?"

"Yes," said Ellen's mother, "She has a pain in her back today. Joy is giving her a treatment. She'll come to the phone soon."

A bit later, "Hello, Ellen, how are you?"
"Oh, I'm fine," her cheery voice answered.

"Fine, even with a pain in your back?"

Dear Ellen, she has learned secret inward contentment and happiness because she knows God is in control.

Ellen was born with an open spine. Correct medical care should have taken care of the problem. But the doctor gave this little baby the wrong medicine. Her spine healed outwardly, but inside an infection caused a build-up of pus. This left Ellen slighty crippled.

As a child, Ellen was full of life and energy. She ran and played with her lively brothers and sisters. She could do nearly everything they did, but when they had such fun running races, Ellen always lagged behind.

One day at school the children were playing 7-Up. Ellen tagged a playmate who yelled, "The crippled girl touched me!" Ellen was sad and a little angry. "I'm Ellen, not the crippled girl," she thought. She told her mom about it that evening. Mom held her close and gently explained. "You are crippled, honey, but we love you so dearly. You are special just as you are. God has work for you to do."

Later, Ellen's family moved to Belize. Ellen was a missionary and a wonderful worker for God who loved her so much. She kept busy by teaching school, Sunday School, sewing for others, and cheering people with lovely art work.

Today, Ellen teaches school in Pennsylvania. She manages her classroom very well, though she walks with a cane. Her students call her Miss Ellen, and they love and respect her. I believe some will grow up to be missionaries and other workers for God because of her sweet influence.

You too are special, just as you are!

Treasure Search

The Lord thy God in the midst of thee is mighty; he will save, he will rejoice over thee with joy; he will rest in his love, he will joy over thee with singing.

Zephaniah 3:17

READ ISAIAH 43:21 AND ACTS 13:36

Consequences

Search me , O God,

and know my heart:

try me, and know my thoughts.

~Psalm 139:23

Tragedy at the Dance

Honor thy father and mother; which is the first commandment with promise; That it may be well with thee, and thou mayest live long on the earth. –Ephesians 6:2-3

On New Year's Eve in 1881, a twilight glow softly enshrouded the peaceful farmstead of John and Eliza Neff of Sugarcreek, Ohio. The evening chores were completed and now the family had retired for the night.

"John," said Eliza, "I am grateful Mary went to bed without saying more about going to the dance at the K.P. Hall in Shanesville. I'm thankful, too, that you forbade her to go. I fear for Mary. Her utmost heart's desire is not to please the Lord. We must be diligent in prayer for her."

Meanwhile, Mary was in her bedroom upstairs. All was quiet, except for one thing. Her mind was not at peace; rather, the tempter who had been speaking to her all day, continued, "Your parents are too strict and religious. Dunkards are so narrow-minded. You are young only once, Mary. Go enjoy yourself this night. What could be wrong with a little music and fun?"

Mary yielded to the tempter's voice. Quietly she got out of bed. She slipped open her window and went out on the back porch roof. The cold and beauty of the moonlit snowy landscape nearly took her breath away. Not even a barking dog disturbed her escape.

The two-mile walk to town was lonely and a bit scary. She nearly wished she hadn't come, but when she saw the lamps of the hall glowing and heard the gay music, her footsteps quickened.

The evening fun seemed much better than being at home, until suddenly there was an ominous crackling sound as vibrations from the dance and the weight of the many people on the old wooden floor made it crack and break in the middle. Terrified screams filled the air as many people slid and fell to their deaths in the basement below. The old coal stove and barrels of oil soon burst into flames. The gay dance was transformed into a hideous burning of tortured bodies.

Mary managed to escape the burning hall, but her feet were badly burned. Terrified, she ran for home. Halfway there, she collapsed and later was found by the road frozen and dead.

Her parents could only hope that Mary had cried to God for mercy and pardon as she lay there dying.

Sin will take you farther than you want to go.

Treasure Search

Good understanding giveth favor:
but the way of transgressors is hard.

Proverbs 13:15

READ AMOS 2:4 AND PROVERBS 15:5

Do It Right!

And whatsoever ye do, do it heartily, as to the Lord,
and not unto men. ~Colossians 3:23

Whatsoever thy hand findeth to do, do it with thy might.
~Ecclesiastes 9:10

The ten students in second grade class were all working very hard. The classroom was quiet except for pencils scratching. Heads were bent over their desks as the children worked diligently on the math problems.

Mary was working as fast as she could. Her pencil buzzed right along. God had given her a keen mind. She liked math and did careful work most of the time. She was adding and subtracting as fast as she could. Finally she did the last problem. Quickly she took her paper up to the teacher's desk. Just a bit later Jeff was finished with his math too.

Mary sat down with a smug little smile. She loved being the first one done. It made her feel good and smart to beat the class.

Later the teacher was checking the math sheets. She wondered why Mary had a few simple problems wrong and had even forgotten to do three easy problems.

What was happening to Mary? She used to get excellent grades in math. The teacher thought and thought; suddenly she knew. The class was just working way too fast!

They were trying to see who could beat the rest, instead of seeing who could do their BEST!

Whatever your hand finds to do,
Do it with your might;
That means do it diligently
And always right!

Treasure Search

Whatsoever thy hand findeth to do,
do it with thy might; for there is no work,
nor device, nor knowledge, nor wisdom, in
the grave, whither thou goest.

Ecclesiastes 9:10

READ COLOSSIANS 1:10 AND 2 TIMOTHY 2:15

The Garbage Truck

As far as the east is from the west, so far hath he removed our transgressions from us. ~Psalm 103:12

I, even I, am he that blotteth out thy transgressions for mine own sake, and will not remember thy sins ~Isaiah 43:25

Nancy was cleaning out her basement. What a mess it was! Soon it was looking better as she put all the trash in garbage bags. Old tin cans, broken dishes, and other junk—she didn't want to see it again!

Then she brushed down spiders and webs. The floor was soon swept clean also. "Looks much better," she sighed. "Clean, orderly rooms make me feel good."

Later that evening, she had more garbage to pitch in the trash bag: potato peelings, eggshells, orange peels, and the empty cake mix box. Nancy's son, Jack, carried all the trash bags to the end of their lane.

In the morning, the garbage truck workers picked up all the junk. Nancy was glad to see it go, glad she would never see it again. She never once had the urge to run after the truck and yell, "Give me my trash back!"

Is your life full of garbage and trash? Are you bothered by anger, madness, wrong attitudes, disobedience, or pride? Clean up and get rid of it by confessing your wrongs and telling God you are sorry.

God will forgive you. The blood of Jesus cleanses you from sin. You can be happy, pure, and clean!

When sin does cease
How great our peace!

Treasure Search

But if we walk in the light, as he is in the light, we have fellowship one with another, and the blood of Jesus Christ his Son cleanseth us from all sin.

If we confess our sins, he is faithful and just to forgive us our sins, and to cleanse us from all unrighteousness.

1 John 1:7, 9

READ REVELATION 1:5

You Can't Do Wrong and Get By

He revealeth the deep and secret things: he knoweth what is in the darkness, and the light dwelleth with him.
–Daniel 2:22

Some stores have a secret surveillance system, a camera that people cannot see, which watches them as they shop.

One day, a lady went shopping. She was looking for a new pair of shoes. She found a pair she liked. She put them on and looked around. Good, no one was watching! Quickly, she stuck her old shoes in the box, put them on the shelf, and finished her shopping with the new shoes on her feet.

She found a few more things she wanted and went to pay. She wished the clerk a good day and was very polite.

Then she walked to the door, but she was stopped by a security guard. "Ma'am," he said, "you have something you did not pay for."

Suddenly her manners were gone. She got mad. "What do you mean? I have the receipt. I paid for my things." She was tempted to hit him with her purse!

"Lady," he said, "we have you on camera; come and see what you did. If you won't admit it, we have your old shoes. Now, come this way." Sadly, she went with him. She was caught!

God has a much greater surveillance system. He knows what everyone, everywhere, is doing all the time. He gave us laws for our own good. How blest and happy we are when we have nothing to hide.

Write down the two Commandments this lady disobeyed:

1.

2.

Remember to look up.
You can't do wrong and get by.

Treasure Search

Search me, O God, and know my heart: try me, and know my thoughts:

And see if there be any wicked way in me, and lead me in the way everlasting.
Psalm 139:23, 24

READ LUKE 8:17 AND EXODUS 20:15, 16

Hidden Treasure

Yea, the darkness hideth not from thee; but the night shineth as the day: the darkness and the light are both alike to thee. ~Psalm 139:12

Achan was hurrying home to his tent. Anxiously, he looked behind him, then quickly he went through the tent opening. "Hurry, my wife," he said. "Pull aside this rug!" He then stooped, and with a large tool he dug a hole in the ground. "Look here, my dear," he breathed. "We shall be rich at last!" His family watched in awe as he took from a bag a large wedge of gold (worth about 3,000 dollars). It sparkled even in the dim light of the tent. Next came 200 shekels of silver (352 dollars) and a lovely, well-made Babylonian garment. He placed these treasures in the hole and carefully covered them.

There, he sighed with relief as he smoothed the rug back over his hidden treasures. "This is our secret, family of mine, absolutely no one else may know!" he told everyone.

"What a day this has been," he went on. "This morning you know we quietly walked around Jericho seven times. Then

Joshua said, 'Shout!' What a noise that shout made. Then, Jericho's huge thick walls fell down flat with a mighty crash. It was a fearful and awesome sight. We marched into that city and utterly destroyed every living man and beast.

"Joshua had told us to save all the gold and silver, and the vessels of brass and iron for the Lord's treasury; everything else was destroyed and burned! Well, we obeyed, except—he eyed the spot under the rug . . . no one will know I saved the best for us!"

Achan was bone-tired. Nevertheless, he slept fitfully, his slumber troubled with dreams of being found out.

Live so that you have nothing to hide.

Treasure Search

And Samuel said, Hath the Lord as great delight in burnt offerings and sacrifices, as in obeying the voice of the Lord? Behold, to obey is better than sacrifice, and to hearken than the fat of rams.

1 Samuel 15:22

READ EZEKIEL 33:31

Hidden Treasure

Continued

O God, thou art terrible out of thy holy places: the God of Israel is he that giveth strength and power unto his people. Blessed be God. ~Psalm 68:35

For the wages of sin is death, but the gift of God is eternal life through Jesus Christ our Lord. ~Romans 6:23

How foolish it is when man thinks he can hide sin. God is the Father of lights. He can easily search out and reveal any hidden work of darkness and sin.

Now God was angry with the children of Israel because Achan had disobeyed. The Lord would not help them as long as the sin was hidden.

Their next challenge was to capture the small city of Ai. Three thousand men went to battle, but they were defeated, chased home, and thirty-six were killed!

Joshua rent his clothes; he and the other leaders fell to the ground crying out to the Lord for mercy.

At eventide, God told Joshua, "Get up, Israel has sinned, stolen, and lied. I will not be among you anymore unless you destroy the wicked ones. Joshua got up early the next morning. He called each tribe to him. The tribe of Judah was taken. He checked each family till it became known that Achan was the guilty one.

Achan finally confessed when Joshua said, "My son, tell me what thou hast done, hide it not."

Achan said, "I saw, I coveted, I took a Babylonish garment, 200 shekels of silver, and 50 shekels in weight of gold. They are hidden under my tent." Messengers ran and found the treasures.

Achan, his family, and all he owned, including the treasures, were taken out of the valley of Achor. Achan and his family were stoned and then burned.

Once again the blessing of the Lord was with the children of Israel, for sin was no longer in their camp. (From Joshua 6 and 7.)

Achan's treasures were his ruin.

Treasure Search

Every good gift and every perfect gift is from above, and cometh down from the Father of lights, with whom is no variableness, neither shadow of turning.

James 1:17

READ PSALM 66:18 AND JAMES 5:16

The High Cost of Disobedience

Obey them that have the rule over you, and submit yourselves: for they watch for your souls, as they that must give account, that they may do it with joy, and not with grief: for that is unprofitable for you. —Hebrews 13:17

TRAPPED UNDER A TRAIN

Eleven-year-old Tonya and her twelve-year-old brother Rod were having lots of fun riding their bikes, but they were getting bored just riding around home.

"Let's ride down to the train station," Rod yelled. Tonya hesitated. Their dad had forbidden them to ride on the streets, and the train station was two blocks away. Finally, she said, "Let's go, but don't tell Dad!"

Tonya led the way across the railroad overpass. She sped down the ramp to the station. On the way down she clamped her brakes, but alas, she was going too fast and couldn't stop.

"Rod!" she yelled in fright as she plunged to the tracks below.

The engineer of an oncoming train had seen Tonya's wild ride. He knew she would fall. He hit the brake, but the train could not stop in time. Tonya's screams filled the air. She was trapped under the train. One of her legs was severed above the knee, the other leg was caught in a wheel. A young man got off the train. He heard Tonya's cries. Glancing under the train, he saw her tear-filled eyes and crawled under the train to hold her and comfort her until they could get the train jacked up to free her. When she was finally free, a helicopter was there to speed her to the hospital, where she stayed for seven weeks.

Today Tonya is a much older and wiser person. The fact that she is crippled is a constant reminder to herself how important it is to always obey. Sometimes a young person will ask Tonya why she moves about so strangely. She is happy when young children ask, for it gives her an opportunity to tell them about the high cost of disobedience.

Obedience can save you from many snares.

Treasure Search

Children, obey your parents in the Lord: for this is right.

Ephesians 6:1

READ EXODUS 20:12

God Sees All

Pray for us: for we trust we have a good conscience, in all things willing to live honestly. ~Hebrews 13:18

Thou shalt not steal. ~Exodus 20:15

Preacher Paul and his wife were flying to the west coast where he was to conduct a series of revival meetings. As they flew, Paul was studying his Bible.

The stewardess came by and noticed the Bible on Paul's lap. She said, "You don't see many people reading that nowadays!" Paul told her he was studying for a message, one about the conscience.

"Oh," she remarked, "people today have no conscience." She went on to explain, "I have worked for this airline for thirty years and it is getting worse. People take so much from us. They steal the blankets and pillows off the airplanes. One hundred thousand articles are stolen from this airline in a year! Before we land, we ask the people using headsets to pass them to the middle aisle, but many just disappear. Too bad how people have no conscience!"

The stewardess moved on down the aisle. Paul sat there thinking. When the flight neared its end, he heard the announcement, "Pass the headsets to the center aisle." Sure enough, Paul saw one lady stuff her headphones into her purse!

What about you and I?
Oh, we behave when we fly,
But at home with work to do,
Are we obedient and cheerful, too?

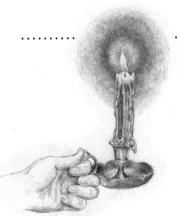

Treasure Search

Recompense to no man evil for evil.
Provide things honest in the sight of all men.

Romans 12:17

READ ROMANS 13:13 AND 1 THESSALONIANS 4:12

Missionaries

*Every where I go the
Lord is always with me.*

Missionaries

Go ye therefore, and teach all nations, baptizing them in the name of the Father, and of the Son, and of the Holy Ghost. ~Matthew 28:19

Also I heard the voice of the Lord, saying, Whom shall I send, and who will go for us? Then said I, Here am I; send me. ~Isaiah 6:8

WHAT IS A MISSIONARY?

First of all, a missionary is someone who loves the Lord very much.

A missionary often goes to lands far away to tell people about Jesus. A missionary loves people and most of all wants them to love Jesus, so they can have peace and joy on earth, and heaven when they die.

A missionary often lives in a village setting with many people living nearby. He may be very busy working and someone will drop by to talk or to request a favor. He always takes time to listen, for he remembers that people are more important than things. He must take time for people, or he defeats the purpose of being a missionary.

A missionary wants most of all to please God in all that he does and says.

Lord, prepare me to be a missionary,
Pure and holy, tried and true.
With thanksgiving I'll be a living
Missionary for you.

Treasure Search

But ye shall receive power, after that the Holy Ghost is come upon you: and ye shall be witnesses unto me both in Jerusalem, and in all Judaea, and in Samaria, and unto the uttermost part of the earth.

Acts 1:8

READ MARK 16:15

A Mission Church

O worship the Lord in the beauty of holiness: fear before him, all the earth. ~Psalm 96:9

I was glad when they said unto me, Let us go into the house of the Lord. ~Psalm 122:1

The doors and windows of the small mission church stood open in the warm tropical climate. Most Sundays found a little brown and white dog in church. He liked his Sunday rest on the cool, bare cement floor. He lay contentedly in the middle aisle. As people came in they merely stepped over or around him. It was quite common to see this dog in church.

Mosquitoes freely attended services—uninvited of course. Little coils (called fish) sat on small stands on the floor. These were lit with a match. The coils smoked to chase away the pests. There were no cars parked outside. Almost everyone walked to church.

I have pleasant memories of worshiping God in that setting. Thankfully it does not take an expensive temple or modern cathedral in which to worship the Lord of heaven and earth. Above all else, God wants our hearts, our love, and our adoration.

The beauty of a church is not in the building, but in the spirit of those who worship there.

Treasure Search

God is greatly to be feared in the assembly of the saints, and to be had in reverence of all them that are about him.

Psalm 89:7

READ JOHN 4:23, 24

Adventures at Night

The righteous cry, and the Lord heareth, and delivereth them out of all their troubles. —Psalm 34:17

I will both lay me down in peace, and sleep: for thou, Lord, only makest me dwell in safety. —Psalm 4:8

Nancy Coblentz awoke with a start. The night was dark, warm, and humid. The outdoor yard light cast dim shadows in her room. "What woke me up?" she wondered groggily.

Then she saw a movement on the floor. First she thought it was a dog wagging its tail. Suddenly, she realized it was a man on his hands and knees crawling into her room. She threw back the covers and screamed. In an instant, the man stood up and ran. Soon he was out the door. The sound of his footsteps faded away in the black night.

Shakily, Nancy got out of bed. Her friend Marilyn woke up with all the commotion. They snapped on the lights and found that the man who had wanted to rob them had cut through the wire mesh of the back screen door to enter the house.

Marilyn's suitcase was out in the living room. It had been taken from her bedroom. The man had been in her room and gone through things while she was sleeping peacefully.

Nancy and Marilyn thanked God for His protection over them that night. They lived in an area that was notorious for robberies, yet they were never harmed.

Life on the mission field in Belize certainly wasn't all calm and peaceful. Yet, because they knew Jesus, the "Prince of Peace," they had courage to face each day and night.

In Jesus there is peace in the midst of storms.

Treasure Search

What time I am afraid, I will trust in thee.

Psalm 56:3

READ ISAIAH 25:4 AND MARK 4:37–41

An Old Man Visits School

Thou shalt rise up before the hoary head, and honor the face of the old man, and fear thy God; I am the Lord.
—Leviticus 19:32

The old man walked up to the school. His hair was gray and his back was bent.

Teacher Jane was quite surprised to see him. Though he lived nearby, he had never before visited this little school in Belize. What could he want? "Come on in," Jane said kindly.

"Thank you, sister," he responded. The old man walked to the front of the class. He looked stern, shook his finger at the children, and said, "I know one of you hid my machete. I need it and want it back today. What would any of us do without a machete? I use it all the time to cut my kindling, chop my grass, and cut up meat and coconuts. Why, I take it along whenever I go walking. I need it now. What if I'd meet up with a poisonous snake?"

All of the children frankly denied hiding the old man's machete. Most of them thought Hank had done it.

What was the teacher to do? She called for the principal, Matt. He called Hank out and they talked about it. Finally, Hank admitted that he had hidden the machete. Hank was spanked for his dishonesty.

Hank was an orphan. He did not have parents who loved him and taught him how to act. At least for now, he had a home. Joe Williams' family had said that Hank could stay with them.

Hank was mad about his spanking. He stalked home and told Joe, "I was spanked for a silly little prank."

You can't do wrong and get by.

Treasure Search

Remember now thy Creator in the days of thy youth, while the evil days come not, nor the years draw nigh, when thou shalt say, I have no pleasure in them.

Ecclesiastes 12:1

READ DANIEL 2:28

An Angry Man
Comes to School

But I say unto you, Love your enemies, bless them that curse you, do good to them that hate you, and pray for them which despitefully use you, and persecute you.
–Matthew 5:44

Matt was busy grading papers after school. He glanced up when he heard footsteps. Joe, a lean, wiry man with a black mustache, was coming. Joe, obviously angry, looked fierce.

"Lord," Matt prayed, "give me your words and wisdom. I wonder what I have done to upset him." He soon found out.

"Matt, you had no business spanking Hank yesterday. He has enough problems. Don't you touch that boy again. I'll take care of him!"

Matt kept calm; he didn't defend himself or argue. He hardly said a word. Joe finally left.

The next evening Matt was enjoying delicious Belizean food at John and Karen's house. They had black tea, powder buns, beans and tortillas. The kindness and love in this home was a balm to his soul after his meeting with Joe the day before. "Thank God, Matt, He kept you safe yesterday when Joe came to school," Karen said. "He had a knife hidden in his clothes. Depending how you would have responded to him, he might have used it."

Matt sat there awhile in stunned silence. "Yes, thank God," he slowly said, "and thanks, Sister Karen, for all this delicious food. If everyone were as kind as you, this world would be much happier!"

Not long after that, Joe got very sick. He needed someone to drive him to the doctor. Only the mission had a vehicle, and Matt was glad to take him. He was thankful God had given him a chance to show kindness to Joe.

God's love in our heart makes us
warm and kind to others.

Treasure Search

If it be possible, as much as lieth in you, live peaceably with all men. Therefore if thine enemy hunger, feed him; if he thirst, give him drink: for in so doing thou shalt heap coals of fire on his head.
Romans 12:18-21

READ PSALM 141:3, JAMES 1:19, AND 1 PETER 3:9, 10

No Home

Can a woman forget her sucking child, that she should not have compassion on the son of her womb? Yea, they may forget, yet will I not forget thee. ~Isaiah 49:15

There was once a little boy with lovely brown curls. He had a sweet, pretty sister, but their parents did not love each other or their children. Their dad moved from Belize to the United States to find work and their mother moved to England.

Dick and Ann went to live with their great-grandparents who were very old, and growing feeble.

Ann had to work hard even though she was only seven years old. Since old Great-Grandma had no washing machine, she scrubbed her clothes by hand. Ann had to do her own in a big bucket or tub.

On Sundays they would walk one mile to a little mission church, where they enjoyed singing and listening to Bible stories.

At school Ann was exceptionally smart and had good manners. Dick was a bit slow and very mischievous.

The old grandfather told Dick's teacher that Dick was hit on the head with a hammer when he was small and as a result he wasn't very bright.

Dick could learn, but the lack of love, plus the neglect, sometimes made him difficult to work with.

Yet, Dick and Ann were sweet and lovable. They would share some of their lunch: hard bread, scrambled eggs, or a bit of cheese. Their teacher always thanked them, but when they weren't looking, she stuck the food away.

Some days, Dick and Ann did not smell good. They had no bathtub at home. At times there were rings of dirt on their necks. They had no mother to keep them clean.

It is easy to take our parents for granted. One of the greatest blessings in life is to have parents who love God, love their children, and make a happy home for them.

Thank God for your loving parents.

Treasure Search

When my father and my mother forsake me, then the Lord will take me up.

Psalm 27:10

READ PSALM 82:3 AND PSALM 146:9

No Home

Continued

A father of the fatherless, and a judge of the widows, is God in his holy habitation. —Psalm 68:5

"Teacher, Teacher," the children rushed into my classroom. "Teacher, Dick is so rude; he was spitting on us."

I called Dick in and explained to him that spitting on people is very rude and unkind. "Do not do it again, or I will spank you."

A few days later Dick was spitting on the children again. I called him into the classroom. "Dick, do you remember what happens now?" Poor Dick started to cry. He would have bolted out the door at a high speed if I had not held tightly to his arm.

Dick received many punishments at school that year: for lying, for cheating, for meanness, and for other offenses. The discipline helped. He learned to do better, but he longed for attention, love, and security at home.

One day, Dick kept pointing to the open school door. His desk was right by the door. I frowned at him; he was to keep at his work. He kept on pointing to the door. Finally I went to look. Just outside, there was a tarantula (a big spider with black, hairy legs and a bright orange body). I was afraid of those spiders. I asked my class, "Does anyone want to kill it?" All the little boys popped up their hands. They weren't afraid of a big spider!

Dick and Ann were still living with their great-grandparents. Occasionally they received a letter from their dad. "We probably won't be in school next year because he'll come for us," they'd say. But he never came.

If you are from a home that is broken or filled with strife, remember your Father in heaven will always love you, and He cares.

God will never let you down.

Treasure Search

For the Lord God will help me;
therefore shall I not be confounded:
therefore have I set my face like a flint,
and I know that I shall not be ashamed.

Isaiah 50:7

READ PSALM 10:14; 82:3

Robbers!

As the mountains are round about Jerusalem, so the Lord is round about his people from henceforth even forever.
~Psalm 125:2

The little black car bumped slowly over the slippery, muddy road. The skies were gray and overcast. What a dreary, rainy day! Miss Ellen was glad to be going home. It had been a long day at the office of her brother's chicken processing plant. Life seemed as dreary as the Belizean weather. Tears spilled down over Ellen's cheeks.

Up ahead, she saw a man beside the road. "Must be a worker carrying some wood home to his family." She slowed down as she contemplated, "Why not stop and give him a ride?"

Then suddenly, Miss Ellen saw five more men charging down the hill toward her car. They looked awful, with black stocking masks over their faces and . . . was that guns they were holding?

Quickly, she pressed down on the gas pedal. The car shot ahead. This enraged the robbers. They were wicked, hard men, and wanted money no matter what. They thought Miss Ellen had a lot of money with her from her office.

They were mad that Miss Ellen hadn't stopped. Wildly, they aimed their guns at the car. Eight to ten shots rang out in the still evening on that lonely country road.

"Oh, Lord," Miss Ellen prayed, "I'm coming home unless you protect me." She was consoled with the thought: Whether living or dying, I am the Lord's!

My times are in thy hand.

Treasure Search

Evening, and morning, and at noon, will I pray, and cry aloud: and he shall hear my voice.

Psalm 55:17

READ EPHESIANS 6:10, 18

Robbers!

Continued

The eternal God is thy refuge, and underneath are the everlasting arms: and he shall thrust out the enemy from before thee. —Deuteronomy 33:27

For to me to live is Christ, and to die is gain. —Philippians 1:21

The bullets hit her car. One went through the roof near her head, another through the door and the front seat, but she was unharmed. Her car spun around, turned back toward the bandits, and jolted to a stop in the ditch. The men ran up, yanked open the car door, and one of them held a gun to her forehead. "You should be dead," one of them snarled. Miss Ellen calmly replied, "Then I'd be with Jesus." She was scared, but felt a calm and peace. She was not afraid to die.

"Where's the money?" the men demanded.

They searched the car, took Miss Ellen's purse and her bag of apples, and left, disappearing into the bushy jungle by the roadside.

Shakily, Miss Ellen crawled out of the car and began to walk the lonely, long mile to her home. "Maybe they'll come after me when they find only a little money in my purse," she worried, "and I cannot even run!" Her thoughts turned heavenward. She sang God Is So Good. She was thankful to be alive and kept on singing all the way home.

What a relief when she finally saw her home up ahead. Home at last—what a haven! She fell sobbing into her mother's arms. "Mother," she gasped, "I am so thankful to be safely home. I was so close to death tonight!" Her mother Orpha cried too, when she heard what had happened. Together they thanked God for His love and protection.

God is with His children.

Treasure Search

Be careful for nothing; but in every thing by prayer and supplication with thanksgiving let your requests be made known unto God.

And the peace of God, which passeth all understanding, shall keep your hearts and minds through Christ Jesus.

Philippians 4:6, 7

READ PSALM 59:16, 17

A Brave Missionary

Finally, my brethren, be strong in the Lord, and in the power of his might. –Ephesians 6:10

God is our refuge and strength, a very present help in trouble. –Psalm 46:1

Mary Slessor sailed from Scotland to Africa in 1876. She lived in wild jungles among savage natives. Mary told them about Jesus and the road to heaven. She worked with great courage and unselfishness.

There were no roads through the jungle—only footpaths. Mary would often travel from village to village over these jungle paths with only one or two companions. Dangerous man-eating leopards lived in the forests.

A friend asked Mary, "How is it that none of those beasts ever attacked you? Are you a kind of Daniel in the lion's den?" Mary laughed and said, "Whenever we travel through leopard country, we keep singing all the time. You just don't know how these people sing! It frightens any decent leopard away into the next valley."

Once a hippopotamus attacked the canoe in which Mary was riding. "Save us!" the paddlers screamed. Although they were strong in their ungodly ways, yet they had much respect for Mary's religion. Mary grabbed a tin basin and slapped at the beast. Its tusks bit the basin, crumpling it with a loud clatter. Startled, the creature grunted and dived out of sight.

For some strange reason, the natives thought that twin babies should not live. They would throw them out in the jungle. Mary rescued many, many twins. People marveled at the number of children she loved and provided for with very little money. She saw many of the twins she saved grow up to be pastors, school teachers, and other godly workers. Every year she continued to save more twins, and sometimes their mothers.

Mary was God's shining light in Africa for nearly forty years. She died and was buried there by the people she dearly loved.

Are you willing to live anywhere for Jesus?

Treasure Search

When thou passest through the waters, I will be with thee; and through the rivers, they shall not overflow thee: when thou walkest through the fire, thou shalt not be burned; neither shall the flame kindle upon thee.

Isaiah 43:2

READ MATTHEW 28:19, 20

Do Good to All Men

Therefore said he unto them, The harvest truly is great, but the laborers are few; pray ye therefore the Lord of the harvest, that he would send forth laborers into his harvest. . . . And heal the sick that are therein, and say unto them, The kingdom of God is come nigh unto you.
~Luke 10:2, 9

"Don Douglas, Don Douglas, Don Douglas!" the happy, energetic Guatemalan children shouted as they raced down the dusty road after the missionary.

It must have been that way when Jesus was on earth and passed through villages and towns. "Jesus, Jesus, Jesus!" the happy children called, as they ran down the dirt roads after Him. Jesus! He always had time for children: time to give them a pat, a smile, or a story. Many of them also knew of someone whom Jesus had healed.

The Guatemalan children liked Don Douglas. He had been in their home to attend to a sick family member. Or, at least, they had heard a story of a sick child, man, or beast that he had helped.

Don Douglas' missionary work included walking miles and miles, uphill, downhill, and over rugged terrain. Often there was no road, merely a footpath, leading to the home of the sick. He would come to a small house made of adobe brick; or in the back country, of cornstalks tied together. The floors were simply dirt. Coming near the house, Don would call out a greeting, "Buenas tardes!" Curious children would peep out of the cracks. Their mother would return the greeting and welcome him to enter. The interior was never well-lit. He wondered where the sick person was. When his eyes adjusted to the dim light, he saw in the back corner a bed, which was held together by four sturdy branches driven into the ground. The frame was branches of twigs or other strong material. On this was the sick person, lying in his dirty blanket.

With God's love and compassion, Don Douglas attended to his needs.

What have you done for someone today?

Treasure Search

So Jesus had compassion on them, and touched their eyes: and immediately their eyes received sight, and they followed him.

Matthew 20:34

READ 1 PETER 3:8

A Busy Day

He that findeth his life shall lose it: and he that loseth his life for my sake shall find it. ~Matthew 10:39

"How nice to have a break from classroom duties," thought May, "yet there is plenty to do. It sure is true that being on the mission field is a lot of ordinary work."

At six o'clock she was up, and had prayed and committed her day to God. Then she began to work.

First there was a huge pile of laundry with sheets from the guest house. Soon the wringer washing machine was busily humming and swishing out the dirt. May hung baskets full of clean laundry up to dry in the fresh morning air.

Next there was a big pile of dishes and some meat jars that needed washing from the previous day's butchering. May sighed and felt a bit overworked. She sternly reminded herself that she was doing this work for the Lord.

May had invited one of her third grade students, Sharon, to help her bake cookies that morning. Soon the delicious smell of molasses and chocolate chip cookies filled her little kitchen.

Sharon was so happy to help. She had probably never baked cookies before. By noon the cookies were all baked. Sharon ran home with a smile on her face and a plate of cookies in her hand.

A neighbor lady came by for a little chat. When she left, May relaxed a while with a book, then went to see a few older ladies in the village.

Later, May was nearly done folding and putting away the laundry when two co-teachers returned from their travels. They were hungry, and they wondered whether May would make some hamburgers and plantain chips for them. May returned to work in the kitchen once more.

That night she was tired and prayed, "Lord, this day was service for others; thank you that it was done as to you! I offer all my service to you. Amen."

Help and be kind to others for Jesus' sake.

Treasure Search

And whosoever shall give to drink
unto one of these little ones a cup of cold
water only in the name of a disciple, verily
I say unto you, he shall in no wise lose his reward.
Matthew 10:42

READ PHILIPPIANS 4:13 AND COLOSSIANS 3:23, 24

A Hard Man

For God so loved the world, that he gave his only begotten Son, that whosoever believeth in him should not perish, but have everlasting life. ~John 3:16

Daniel gave his horse a kick in the ribs. He was a rough cattleman, tall and lean with craggy features.

Now, after caring for his cattle on the open range, Daniel was in a hurry to go home to eat hot food and to rest.

"I want my tea. Now!" Daniel said as he walked into the kitchen. His wife Laura scurried around, busily preparing his food. She fanned the fire on the hearth into brighter flames. Daniel sat impatiently tapping his foot on the floor.

Daniel did not have a good reputation. He used vulgar speech, liked to drink alcohol, and was not always kind to Laura.

The missionaries in his village were told, "Don't waste your time talking to Daniel about the Lord. Forget about him; he's a hard man."

The missionaries, Lester, Sister Nancy, and Esther, were friendly to Daniel and Laura. They showed an interest in their lives and talked to them about Jesus.

The mission school was built across the road from Daniel's house. Esther loved visiting Daniel and Laura after school. Sometimes she went fishing with Laura, or she would go along to help work at their rice plantation.

Don and Laura watched the missionaries. They took note of their kindness and love to everyone. What made them different—so happy and at peace?

The Spirit of God was speaking to the hearts of Daniel and Laura. Laura decided she wanted to live for Jesus. Now she joined in prayer for her husband that he, too, would come to love the Lord.

The love of God can melt the hardest heart.

Treasure Search

Whom we preach, warning every man, and teaching every man in all wisdom; that we may present every man perfect in Christ Jesus.

Colossians 1:28

READ 1 JOHN 1:9 AND ROMANS 5:8

A Hard Man

Continued

Therefore if any man be in Christ, he is a new creature: old things are passed away; behold, all things are become new. ~2 Corinthians 5:17

One Sunday afternoon Esther stopped at Daniel and Laura's house. They had a nice visit and began discussing what it takes to become a Christian. Daniel said, "I am ready to take that step." Laura looked at Daniel in an amazed, unbelieving way and questioned, "Daniel, do you mean that?"

"Yes," he said, "I do mean it. I want to become a child of God!"

Daniel, Laura, and Esther bowed their heads and prayed. It was a sacred moment. Daniel's prayer was simple and heartfelt. "Lord, thank you for loving a sinner like me. I believe you died for my sins. Forgive all my sins, O Lord. Come into my heart. I trust you for my Savior. Amen."

The coming days proved that Daniel really had become a new man. He stopped cursing and drinking. Laura knew he had changed. Now he was kind to her, and he prayed each day.

Daniel and Laura came to love the Bible. They faithfully attended church and prayer meeting. Daniel would often say, "I'm just so thankful that the missionaries came to show us the way to heaven before it was too late!"

The teachers from the mission school enjoyed visiting at Daniel's house. Often they were invited to stay for a meal. Daniel and Laura brightened their days when they felt lonely or discouraged. Their lives shone with God's kindness and love.

God changes men!

Treasure Search

They have addicted themselves to the ministry of the saints,

For they have refreshed my spirit and yours: therefore acknowledge ye them that are such.
1 Corinthians 16:15, 18

READ GALATIANS 6:10

A Faithful Worker

And he that sent me is with me: the Father
hath not left me alone. ~John 8:29

Sister Nancy sighed as she eased her weary frame into the blue hammock. The evening breezes blowing in from the sea felt refreshing after a busy day in warm, humid Belize City.

Thirty years ago when I came to Belize, Central America, I never dreamed I'd stay so long, she mused. I could go back to Ohio, but there's work to do here. God called me here, and I will stay until he calls me elsewhere. I do love the work I can do for Jesus: visiting ladies in prison, counseling the sad, hurt, and needy, and conducting children's hour for the neighborhood. Many of these children come from unhappy homes—shacks filled with evil, unfaithfulness, and darkness.

How much these people need Jesus—JESUS!—the only true light. Sister Nancy's mind traveled far as darkness settled over the city.

Was it actually twenty years that I taught school in Hattieville? And think of all the countless visitors who passed through each year. I enjoyed showing hospitality to them, though often it made extra work.

Here I am, already sixty-seven years old, and God has blessed me with many sons and daughters—Belizeans I have pointed to Jesus and nurtured in the faith. What a precious family they are! On Sunday evening, seven former students were baptized. Their love for the Lord radiated on their youthful faces . . . truly that is fruit of my labor. How I rejoice, and give all praise and honor to God.

"Lord," Sister Nancy prayed, "How I need you each day to continue to be a light in this dark world. Thank you for your daily guidance over the years: Your love, protection, and help. Truly, I am your humble servant; without you, I can do nothing. Keep me near you each day, Father.

"Good night."

Think! Only one life, 'twill soon be past,
Only what's done for Christ will last.

Treasure Search

And I will very gladly spend and be spent for you.

2 Corinthians 12:15

READ JOHN 9:4 AND 2 CORINTHIANS 4:15

I

Thou shalt have no
other gods before thee.

II

Thou shalt not make unto
thee any graven image.

III

Thou shalt not take the
name of the Lord
thy God in vain.

IV

Remember the sabbath
day to keep it holy.

V

Honour they father
and thy mother.

VI

Thou shalt not kill.

VII

Thou shalt not
commit adultery.

VIII

Thou shalt not steal.

IX

Thou shalt not
bear false witness.

X

Thou shalt not covet.

———————

– Exodus 20

The Ten Commandments

Oh! How I love Thy law.

The Ten Commandments

Behold, I set before you this day a blessing and a curse; A blessing, if ye obey the commandments of the Lord your God, which I command you this day: And a curse, if ye will not obey the commandments of the Lord your God. —Deuteronomy 11:26-28

The Ten Commandments were given to Moses by Jehovah God. Whenever people follow God's laws, it is a blessing to them and spares them from many a heartache. God loves us. He redeemed us. He has the right to tell us how to live.

The Ten Commandments teach reverence and respect for God and for our fellowman. The first four commandments are about our relationship with God. The last six are about relating to our fellowman.

Can you recite the Ten Commandments? In a survey that was taken by the American Rights Coalition, less than one percent of teens and adults in Bible churches could name the Ten Commandments.

How sad to neglect the family values that God intends parents to display and teach to their children. Yet, how can we teach them, if we don't know them? How can we afford to neglect God's Word, which we profess to love and follow?

God gave the Ten Commandments for our safety, protection, and good. Yet, how many of us are willing to obey them?

Will you love and obey God's laws?

Treasure Search

And thou shalt teach them diligently unto thy children, and shalt talk of them when thou sittest in thine house, and when thou walkest by the way, and when thou liest down, and when thou risest up.

Deuteronomy 6:7

READ PROVERBS 4:20–22

The Ten Commandments

Continued

This book of the law shall not depart out of thy mouth; but thou shalt meditate therein day and night, that thou mayest observe to do according to all that is written therein: for then thou shalt make thy way prosperous, and then thou shalt have good success. ~Joshua 1:8

In March 1994, a framed copy of the Ten Commandments was ordered removed from a courthouse in Cobb County, Tennessee. Following this, the American Rights Coalition conducted a survey in Cobb County. They found that among the fifteen bookstores, fifteen Christian schools, and twenty churches in the county, only one of each had a copy of the Ten Commandments on public display.

On July 1, 1994, they printed 50,000 copies of the Ten Commandments and distributed them to the churches in Cobb County. Now they are on display in businesses, restaurants, offices, stores, homes, schools, and churches all over the county. Millions of people can see them now, whereas before, only a few saw them on the obscure courthouse wall.

What was meant for evil when someone removed the Ten Commandments from the courthouse, God turned to good!

God's people love His law.

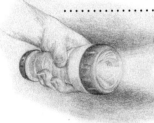

Treasure Search

For this purpose the Son of God was manifested, that he might destroy the works of the devil.

1 John 3:8

READ GENESIS 50:20 AND ISAIAH 61:3

I.
Thou shalt have no other gods before me

Thou shalt love the Lord thy God with all thy heart, and with all thy soul, and with all thy mind.
~Matthew 22:37

You might say,
How does this commandment apply today?
We have no idols in our home.
We're not kneeling down and praying
To a little figure made of stone.
We don't bow to a sun or moon god.
We go to church each Sunday.
We love our Father in heaven,
The one Supreme and only TRUE God.

WHERE IS YOUR HEART?

Kathy liked to read. She read whenever she could. Her mom had a problem getting her away from books long enough to help with the housework.

Yet Kathy seldom read the Bible, even though she knew it was God's message to her. She thought other books were much more exciting. Romance and mystery stories were her favorites.

•   •   •

Harold was a busy man. He liked to work. He went to work early and got home after his little boys were tucked in bed. His family was well provided for. They had a lovely house, the best minivan, and expensive clothes that were always in style.

But did Harold have time to read the Bible and pray with his family? Very seldom.

Do you truly love God?
Or do you love money and things more than God?

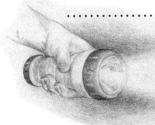

Treasure Search

And he is the head of the body,
the church: who is the beginning, the
firstborn from the dead; that in all things
he might have the preeminence.

Colossians 1:18

READ DEUTERONOMY 6:5

II.
Thou shalt not make unto thee any graven image

That at the name of Jesus every knee should bow, of things in heaven, and things in earth, and things under the earth. And that every tongue should confess that Jesus Christ is Lord, to the glory of God the Father.
~Philippians 2:10, 11

God alone is worthy of our adoration. We shall not bow our knee to any other.

THE LOVE OF MONEY

Janice was a very busy wife and mother. She liked to make and sell quilts. She enjoyed taking pies and crafts to a market. She was so busy that her children aggravated her nerves and got in her way.

She seldom had time to really enjoy her family and make their home a haven of rest and peace.

When Janice sat in church, her mind focused on how much money she had made that week. Frankly, Janice loved money, and money was not making her home happy.

Are eternal values of utmost importance to you?

Treasure Search

For the love of money is the root of all evil: which while some coveted after, they have erred from the faith, and pierced themselves through with many sorrows.

1 Timothy 6:10

READ MATTHEW 13:22 AND EXODUS 20:4, 5

III.
Thou shalt not take the name of the Lord thy God in vain

Not every one that saith unto me, Lord, Lord, shall enter into the kingdom of heaven; but he that doeth the will of my Father which is in heaven. ~Matthew 7:21

HAVE YOU MISUSED GOD'S NAME?

"Rosa is such a good maid," Amanda sighed. "It is hard to see her leave, yet I'm so thankful that she is getting married to such a dedicated Christian man.

"She recommended Maria for our next maid. What do you think, Roman? Maria is from another village; her dad is a minister, and I've been told Maria loves the Lord."

Maria was hired to be Roman and Amanda's house maid. She was a good worker, but she wore very short dresses. So Roman and Amanda decided to have all their maids wear white uniforms.

Amanda found some nice white fabric. She was singing softly as she cut out the dresses and began to sew. Before she was done, she went with Roman on a few errands.

A few days later she came back to her sewing. When she picked up the skirt, she noticed a few smudgy pencil marks around the bottom. The skirt seemed short. I'm sure I cut it longer, Amanda mused. Why, someone must have cut it shorter. Surely not Maria, if she is a Christian!

Amanda asked Maria about it. "Oh, no," Maria said, "I didn't touch that white fabric."

"What shall we do now, Roman?" Amanda asked. After praying about the matter, they decided to draw lots, believing that God would reveal to them whether or not Maria was truthful.

So, with Maria's consent, they took two books and placed fabric in one of them. When Maria came into the room, Roman led in prayer, "Lord, you know all hearts. Nothing is hid from you. Guide Maria's hand and reveal to us the truth."

Maria seemed confident as she chose one of the books. But when she opened it, there was the fabric. She cried and cried and confessed that she had cut the skirt and thrown the cut-off pieces on the garbage truck.

Roman prayed with her and assured her of their love and forgiveness. Maria seemed broken.

Now Maria could choose—to truly live for God and be honest, with nothing to hide, or to go back to her village and live just as she pleased.

A few days later, Maria chose to return to her home.

Those who say they are Christians, yet live dishonestly, take God's name in vain.

Treasure Search

This people draweth nigh unto me with their mouth, and honoureth me with their lips; but their heart is far from me.

Matthew 15:8

READ 1 JOHN 3:18

IV.
Remember the Sabbath day to keep it holy

Six days thou shalt work, but on the seventh day thou shalt rest: in earing time and in harvest thou shalt rest.
~Exodus 34:21

DON'T COME ON THE SABBATH

Nehemiah was a great man of prayer, action, courage, and perseverance. He was the governor of Judah. He encouraged the people to love the Lord and to obey His laws.

One Sabbath day, Nehemiah saw something that grieved his heart. Some of the people were treading their wine-presses; others were bringing in sheaves from the field and loading up their donkeys with wine, grapes, figs, and all manner of burdens. Didn't these people know God's law? Then, too, he saw merchants, hawkers, and peddlers from Tyre in Jerusalem with fish and all kinds of things to sell on the Sabbath.

Nehemiah went to the city rulers, saying, "You are allowing the people to work, buy, and sell on the Sabbath. Because you didn't use your power to stop it, it is as if you were doing it, even though you didn't carry corn or buy fish. You are guilty! Take warning, keep the Sabbath holy, or you will bring God's wrath on Israel!"

Nehemiah ordered the city gates to be shut the evening before the Sabbath and not to be opened again until the morning after. He set some of his trusted servants to guard the gates. Once or twice, after the gates were shut, the merchants approached with their wares. They were denied entrance and so they camped outside the wall. Nehemiah confronted them, "Why do you spend the night here with your things? If you come again, I will lay hands on you." After that warning the merchants didn't come again on the Sabbath day. (From Nehemiah 13:15–22)

Obey God's laws and you will be blessed!

Treasure Search

If thou turn away thy foot from the sabbath, from doing thy pleasure on my holy day; and call the sabbath a delight, the holy of the Lord, honourable; and shalt honour him, not doing thine own ways, nor finding thine own pleasure, nor speaking thine own words:

Then shalt thou delight thyself in the Lord; and I will cause thee to ride upon the high places of the earth, and feed thee with the heritage of Jacob thy father: for the mouth of the Lord hath spoken it.

READ EXODUS 31:15, 17

Isaiah 58:13, 14

IV.
Remember the Sabbath day to keep it holy

Continued

How much then is a man better than a sheep? Wherefore it is lawful to do well on the sabbath days.
–Matthew 12:12

And he saith unto them, Is it lawful to do good on the sabbath days, or to do evil? To save life, or to kill? But they held their peace. –Mark 3:4

DO GOOD ON THE SABBATH

The faraway green hills and mountains of Guatemala looked cool and inviting from the city with all its bustle and noise. But in the mountains life was hard. The fields and gardens were on steep mountain slopes. The roads were bumpy and muddy. For many miles there were no doctors and no cars. Most of the people were poor, caught in poverty's grip and, worse yet, trapped in a false religion, a mixture of Catholicism and witchcraft. The people live, work, and die. Does anyone care? Who will tell them about Jesus?

A young man named Don Douglas came with his wife into those mountains to share the message of God's love.

Don was a veterinarian. Here in the mountains he treated animals and people. The sick people needed help and had no one else to turn to.

On Sunday morning, the Christians gathered for worship at the home of one of the Christian believers. "Oh, day of rest and gladness. The day to worship the Lord God and turn our minds toward heaven. The day to rest from our labors." Sunday was often a busy day for Don Douglas. Some days he preached in the morning and evening. And the sick people asked for help on Sunday, too.

One Sunday afternoon the storekeeper came. "My daughter is ill. Can you help?"

Don Douglas walked to their house. The girl was in need of medical help immediately. Since the case was too difficult for him, Don drove her to Guatemala City Hospital that evening. The roads were hazardous and rough. In one hour and twenty minutes, they were there. Don had done what he could.

Focus on doing good on Sunday.

Treasure Search

And the ruler of the synagogue answered with indignation, because that Jesus had healed on the sabbath day, and said unto the people, There are six days in which men ought to work: in them therefore come and be healed, and not on the sabbath day.

The Lord then answered him, and said, Thou hypocrite, doth not each one of you on the sabbath loose his ox or his ass from the stall, and lead him away to watering?

And ought not this woman, being a daughter of Abraham, whom Satan hath bound, lo, these eighteen years, be loosed from this bond on the sabbath day?

Luke 13:14–16

READ ISAIAH 58:13

V.
Honor thy father and thy mother

My son, hear the instruction of thy father, and forsake not the law of thy mother. ~Proverbs 1:8

Honor = To show respect to
     to regard courteously
     to please and obey
     to be the comfort of your parents

WE WILL OBEY

The wine glimmered and sparkled in the bowls Jeremiah set on the table. It looked tempting and would be refreshing.

And now Jeremiah was offering wine to the Rechabite families. God had said, "Take them to the temple and give them wine to drink."

But they flatly refused the wine. "No, we don't drink wine. Our forefather Jonadab commanded us to never drink wine! He said, 'Obey, and you will live a long, good life in your land.' We have obeyed, and never touched wine to our lips. Our wives, sons, and daughters obey too, and we will not drink wine now!"

The Lord said to Jeremiah, "Go tell the men of Judah and Jerusalem, 'Learn a lesson from the Rechabites. Consider their example; the blessing of the Lord is upon them because they are obedient. But I, God Almighty, have spoken to you again and again. You don't listen, obey, or even pay attention. Evil and disaster will come upon you.

"'But the Rechabites who have obeyed their father in every respect, will always have descendants who will worship and serve me.'" (From Jeremiah 35)

Obedience results in blessings!

Treasure Search

Hearken unto thy father that begat thee, and despise not thy mother when she is old. . . .

The father of the righteous shall greatly rejoice: and he that begetteth a wise child shall have joy of him.

Thy father and thy mother shall be glad, and she that bare thee shall rejoice.

Proverbs 23:22, 24, 25

READ EPHESIANS 6:2, 3

VI.

Thou shalt not kill

Ye have heard that it was said by them of old time, Thou shalt not kill; and whosoever shallkill shall be in danger of the judgment. ~Matthew 5:21

FOLLOWING THE PRINCE OF PEACE

War clouds darkened the beautiful Shenandoah Valley. More Mennonites lived in this prosperous, peaceful farming region of Virginia than in any other Southern State. What would they do when the call came for men to take up arms and fight?

The Mennonites believed that the Gospel of Christ is the way of peace. They held dear the words of Jesus, "Love your enemies and do good to those who hate you." Their goal was to follow Jesus, the Prince of Peace, who prayed for His persecutors. They believed that true Biblical nonresistance was a matter of obedience to the teachings of Jesus who said, "My kingdom is not of this world; if my kingdom were of this world, then would my servants fight. . . ."

The Civil War began in the spring of 1861. The Confederate government commanded the militia and all able-bodied men between the ages of 18 and 45 years of age to come and take up arms. This included the Mennonites. A few of the Mennonites obeyed the summons. Many went into hiding in the mountains and forests. Some chose to stay at home and simply await the outcome. They decided that if they must join the army, none of them would fight.

Christian Good, a dedicated young man, was forced into the army. But he had made a promise to his widowed mother that he would never fire a gun at anyone. He remained true to his promise. In the first battle, he was discovered and reported to a higher officer. He was then charged with disboedience to orders, and the officer in command threatened him with court martial and death if his disobedience was repeated. Still, he would not shoot in any of the battles that followed. Other young men, seeing Christian's courage, also laid down their weapons.

The threats against him were never carried out. He was re-leased on the payment of $500. Quite a number of other men had similar experiences. The church paid for their exemptions. Christian Good worked two years on a farm to repay his fine. He continued to follow Jesus, the Prince of Peace, and later became a faithful minister of the Gospel of Jesus Christ.

Resource: Hartzler, J. S., Mennonites in the World War (Mennonite Publishing House, Scottdale, PA, 1921), pg. 32-34.

Be a person of integrity; stand up for the right.

Treasure Search

My kingdom is not of this world; if my kingdom were of this world, then would my servants fight, that I should not be delivered to the Jews: but now is my kingdom not from hence.

John 18:36

READ MATTHEW 5:44.

VII.
Thou shalt not commit adultery

But whoso committeth adultery with a woman lacketh understanding; he that doeth it destroyeth his own soul.
~Proverbs 6:32

MIKE'S HARD LIFE

To commit adultery is to break your marriage vows.

A happy little girl went running around the house to her daddy. He was talking with Mike. But he had time to give her a hug—and soon she ran off, her braids flying along behind her.

"You know," Mike said, "seeing your little girl like that just breaks my heart . . . I have a little girl, too—but I so seldom see her."

Mike had grown up in the home of an aunt who loved the Lord. From the time he was a small boy, he went to church every Sunday. He loved to sing and hear Bible stories. He knew about Jesus and what he must do if he wanted heaven to be his home someday.

But alas, Mike turned his back on the call of Jesus. When he was fifteen, he left Belize and moved to the United States. There he chose bad company and enjoyed a carefree lifestyle of drinking, smoking, playing cards, partying, and being with ungodly women.

Later, Mike got married. He and his wife had a sweet baby girl, but problems came to this home built on sand. Stormy winds shook their love. They needed Jesus, the Rock, to hold onto. Mike left his wife Ryney. Sometimes he was haunted by words from Scripture. He knew divorce was wrong. Someday he hoped to get back with his wife. Still, he loved parties, drinking, and other women. He was lonely and moved in with a teenage girl. They decided to live together, but not to marry.

The Bible says that this is living in adultery. All who do so cannot inherit the kingdom of heaven. Be not deceived, God's Word never changes.

Determine to obey God's Word.

Treasure Search

So then if, while her husband liveth, she be married to another man, she shall be called an adulteress: but if her husband be dead, she is free from that law; so that she is no adulteress, though she be married to another man. Romans 7:3

READ HEBREWS 11:24, 25, MARK 10:9–12, AND MATTHEW 5:32

VIII.
Thou shalt not steal

Let him that stole steal no more: but rather let him labour, working with his hands the thing which is good, that he may have to give to him that needeth. ~Ephesians 4:28

THOU GOD SEEST ME

To steal is to take what belongs to another.

A small boy and his father were driving through the countryside. They passed neat, well-kept farms, cattle in green pastures, and lush fields of hay and produce.

They came to a field of watermelons. The melons looked big, juicy, ripe, and tempting.

Dad stopped the car. He got out and looked all around. Seeing no one, he said, "Sonny, we will have ourselves a treat!" He bent down to pick a melon, but suddenly he paused, for his son's clear little voice was calling, "Daddy, Daddy, you forgot to look up!"

The man was ashamed. His conscience was pricked. He left the melons and they went on their way.

Perhaps, this boy had a mother who taught him God's Word and took him to Sunday school each Sunday, while his dad preferred to stay at home, rest, and read the paper.

You can hide nothing from God.

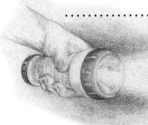

Treasure Search

And she called the name of the Lord
that spake unto her, Thou God seest me:
for she said, Have I also here looked after
him that seeth me?

Genesis 16:13

READ MARK 10:19

IX.
Thou shalt not bear false witness

Lying lips are abomination to the Lord: but they that deal truly are his delight. ~Proverbs 12:22

Wherefore putting away lying, speak every man truth with his neighbour: for we are members one of another. ~Ephesians 4:25

WOLF! WOLF!

Years and years ago, a boy named John watched his father's sheep each day as they grazed on a high hill. He had to guard the sheep from the hungry wolves.

John grew tired of watching the sheep all alone day after day. So one morning, he suddenly screamed, "Wolf! Wolf!"

People in the village below heard his cry. They raced up the hill with brooms, axes, sticks, hoes, and rakes to beat off the wolves. They found no wolf, only John laughing. "I was so lonely," he said. "It's just a joke!"

The kind villagers warned John, "Do not cry 'Wolf' again, unless there are wolves. We are too busy for nonsense!"

John was ashamed and thought he would not trick them again. But in a few days he was ever so bored and lonely.

He cried, "Wolf! Wolf!" The villagers hurried to help him. Again there was no wolf, only John laughing with glee. "Ho, ho! You looked so funny running up the hill!"

The villagers were very angry. "We have work to do!" they shouted. "You will be sorry if you ever trick us again."

Two weeks passed and one day a hungry, cruel wolf really did come. John trembled with fear. He tried to beat off the wolf, but he could not do it alone.

"Wolf! Wolf!" he bellowed. His cries were heard in the village below. No help came. The people thought, John will not trick us three times!

The wolf killed ten fine sheep and lambs. John was crying when he took the rest of the sheep home. He knew he would never again cry 'Wolf!' without good reason.

Honesty always pays.

· ·

Treasure Search

These six things doth the Lord hate: yea, seven are an abomination unto him:

A proud look, a lying tongue, and hands that shed innocent blood,

An heart that deviseth wicked imaginations, feet that be swift in running to mischief,

A false witness that speaketh lies, and he that soweth discord among brethren.

Proverbs 6:16–19

READ PROVERBS 13:5

· ·

X.
Thou shalt not covet

For the love of money is the root of all evil: which while some coveted after, they have erred from the faith, and pierced themselves through with many sorrows.
–1 Timothy 6:10

THE GREEDY KING

Ahab was a very rich and prosperous king of Israel, yet he wanted more, more, and more.

Naboth was Ahab's neighbor. He had a vineyard close to Ahab's palace. Ahab thought that vineyard would be a perfect spot for a garden. His heart was set on having it, so he asked Naboth to sell it or to exchange it for a better vineyard elsewhere.

Now, this vineyard had been in Naboth's family for many years. He would not consider selling it.

Ahab stalked home angrily and, like a pouting child who cannot have his own way, he flopped on his bed, sulking and refusing to eat.

His wife, Jezebel, entered the room. "Why are you so sad? Why won't you eat?" she asked.

"It's all because of Naboth," Ahab whined. "I want his vineyard and he won't sell it!"

"Is this how a king should act?" Jezebel asked. "Get up, eat, drink, and be merry; I will get that vineyard for you."

She arranged for wicked men to lie about Naboth, saying he had blasphemed God and the king. Then she gave orders to have Naboth taken out and stoned to death!

All went as Jezebel planned. Ahab got his vineyard, but when he went to check it out, God sent His prophet Elijah to meet him in the vineyard. He let him know that God had seen all that had happened.

Ahab and his wife would be punished because they had done this evil deed.

It is very important always to be honest and never to take advantage of others. (From 1 Kings 21.)

The way to be happy is to be kind and good!

Treasure Search

Mortify therefore your members which are upon the earth; fornication, uncleanness, inordinate affection, evil concupiscence, and covetousness, which is idolatry: For which thing's sake the wrath of God cometh on the children of disobedience.
Colossians 3:5, 6

READ 1 CORINTHIANS 6:9, 10

Virtues

Purity

Come now, and let us reason together, saith the Lord: though your sins be as scarlet, they shall be as white as snow; though they be red like crimson, they shall be as wool. ~Isaiah 1:18

GOD'S LOVELY SNOW

Softly and silently the snow glided gently down on a sleeping world wrapped in the darkness of night. It covered all the mud and the old brown leaves on the grass. Everything was wrapped in a cozy white blanket of snow!

In the morning, the children's eyes were eager, happy, and enchanted with all the beauty and thoughts of fun in the snow.

Soft, wet snow clung to bushes and trees. It made little snowmen and balls as the happy children played and sledded. What fun it was, this gift of snow!

GOD'S PURE, CLEAN CHILDREN

Sometimes we say unkind words, do naughty things, or act rudely. Then we feel sad, mean, and actually dirty inside. First John 1:7 says Jesus' blood cleanseth us from all sin.

When we tell Jesus we're sorry for all the naughty, wrong things we did, His blood makes us clean. He forgives us, and we can try again. Remember the song, "What can wash away my sins? Nothing but the blood of Jesus."

Treasure Search

Create in me a clean heart, O God;
and renew a right spirit within me.

Psalm 51:10

READ PSALM 51:7

Gracious Old Age

She openeth her mouth with wisdom; and in her tongue is the law of kindness. ~Proverbs 31:26

Remember now thy Creator in the days of thy youth, while the evil days come not, nor the years draw nigh, when thou shalt say, I have no pleasure in them. ~Ecclesiastes 12:1

Agnes Nipples is ninety years old. She lives in a nursing home and is blessed with fairly good health and a clear mind. She could spend her days complaining about living in a nursing home, but she does not.

If you would meet her, you would soon see that she is in the habit of being thankful. Her days are spent beaming at those around her and making them happy with her kind words. Children just love her. She attracts them like a magnet attracts metal!

A friend, Mrs. King, once gave Agnes a few small geraniums. Several years later, Mrs. King went to the nursing home with some schoolchildren to sing. Agnes found Mrs. King and then pointed to two lovely, tall pink geraniums. She explained that they were the ones Mrs. King had given her.

Agnes doesn't forget kindness and she expresses her thankfulness. What Agnes is today at ninety years of age, has been a lifetime developing.

Do you think you will ever be old? What kind of man or woman do you want to be then?

If we desire to be gracious in old age, we had better start practicing now.

Treasure Search

A gracious woman retaineth
honour: and strong men retain riches.

Proverbs 11:16

READ PROVERBS 16:24 AND PHILIPPIANS 4:8

Patience

For he that will love life, and see good days, let him refrain his tongue from evil, and his lips that they speak no guile. ~1 Peter 3:10

FUN IN THE TUB

Margretta and I laughed and giggled in the bathroom where Mother had left us two little girls to play and soak in a warm tub of water.

Soon Mother wondered what was so funny. She was busy getting ready for visitors, but when she came to investigate, what a sight she saw! Margretta (age 1) had a little Tupperware pitcher and was happily dumping water out on the floor. I was slipping and sliding in the water on the floor. Mother looked tired and was cross. Our laughter and giggles were suddenly stifled as we saw Mother's face and took the scolding she gave us.

Later Mother could laugh a bit at our childish innocence and then kindly told us that the floor is not the place to dump the water. She said it would have been better to dump the water into the tub instead of outside the tub.

We decided to keep the water inside the tub next time.

Happy play doesn't have to be messy.

Treasure Search

Wherefore seeing we also are
compassed about with so great a cloud
of witnesses, let us lay aside every weight,
and the sin which doth so easily beset us, and let us
run with patience the race that is set before us.

Hebrews 12:1

READ 2 PETER 1:5–8

Is God Smiling?

Blessed are the peacemakers: for they shall be called the children of God. ~Matthew 5:9

Thou God seest me. ~Genesis 16:13

Think about God as you work and play . . . Is God smiling?

A STICK FIGHT

Two children, Peter and Sue, went out in their yard to pick up the sticks and branches that had blown down during a bad storm. They put the branches on a big pile beside the lane.

Sue started a small pile to carry over to the big pile later. Peter came along and got the biggest stick from Sue's pile. Sue grabbed the other end and said, "That's my stick." They pulled and pulled, then hollered and yelled.

Mother was in the house rocking their little brother who was sick. She heard their yells and went to investigate. This is what

Mother saw: Peter and Sue trying hard to pull that stick away from each other.

"Let Peter have the stick," Mother said. "Be glad he is helping you."

Angrily, Sue suddenly let go. Peter fell to the ground with a thud and a fresh wail of tears. He ran to Mother. "I want to go inside," he wailed. "I don't feel well!"

"OK," said Mother, "but you have to lie on the loveseat because of the fuss." He decided to run back out and happily helped to finish the job.

Later, Peter and Sue had to sit on chairs, while Mother talked with them about being peacemakers and asked what they could have done to make peace.

Peter said he could have just let Sue have her stick. Sue said she should have let Peter take it! Mother said, "Remember to be loving and kind, then you can be happy."

It takes kindness to make peace.

Treasure Search

But the wisdom that is from above
is first pure, then peaceable, gentle, and
easy to be intreated, full of mercy and
good fruits, without partiality, and without hypocrisy.
James 3:17

READ 2 CHRONICLES 16:9, ROMANS12:18, AND PSALM 133:1

Faithfulness

As thy days so shall thy strength be.
~Deuteronomy 33:25

And the men did the work faithfully.
~2 Chronicles 34:12

Strong young Andy bent to pick up his little girl. Happily she clung to him as he gave her a merry ride on his shoulders. Her little giggles were like music in the evening air.

Another evening, a thunderstorm was brewing. Black angry clouds filled the sky. The lightning flashed and the thunder rolled. Little Mary shivered with fright. Quickly she ran to her daddy. He held her safe and secure until the storm had passed.

Many years flew by. What changes the years bring! Mary's father, once so strong, was growing old and feeble. He had Parkinson's disease and needed a lot of care. Wearily, he turned on his bed. His back hurt. His daughter Mary came in so efficient and cheerful. She washed his face and rubbed his back. He was cheered by her joyful spirit.

When she left the room, his mind traveled back in time, forty years before to scenes of long ago. Ah, those happy days when he was young and strong, working hard, faithfully providing for his family. Their home knew hard work, yet it was filled with love and laughter and children—the ever energetic children!

Now those precious children were caring for him. Thankfulness welled up in Andy's heart. Mary was living at home and did her best to care for her parents by cooking meals, doing the laundry, and cleaning the house. The other children took their turn too.

Andy had had Parkinson's disease for 20 years. He had needed extensive care for his last five years. Faithfully, his family did what they could for him. Andy was longing for heaven and perfect rest, when he died at 82.

He and his wife Edna had lived and worked together in love and peace for sixty-two years!

What an example of faithful love!

Treasure Search

But he that shall endure unto the end,
the same shall be saved.

Matthew 24:13

READ 2 CORINTHIANS 12:9 AND LUKE 16:10

Frogs, Grasshoppers, and Smarties

And be ye kind one to another, tenderhearted, forgiving one another, even as God for Christ's sake hath forgiven you.
~Ephesians 4:32

One day two girls and their grandmother came to my house. We were having a nice little chat, until Tinsly found a frog. She grabbed the frog and held it out to Marcy! Marcy was so scared of frogs, she slid off her chair, and sat under the table and cried. Too bad, how troublemakers like to make children cry!

A group of boys were playing nicely together while their mothers were quilting. Suddenly, Sam saw a fat green grasshopper go hopping by. Quickly he grabbed it. He poked the grasshopper at Tom. Tom didn't like grasshoppers and was scared. He quickly jumped away, and nearly cried. Sam kept teasing Tom with the grasshopper until Mom came and made peace.

Three-year-old Margretta was happily sharing some smarties with her little brother and his friend. When there was only one small smartie left, she ran into the house to get a knife to cut the last one in half so the boys could each have one more piece.

What a nice way to keep the peace! The way to be happy is to share.

Are you a peacemaker or a troublemaker?

Treasure Search

Charity suffereth long, and is kind; charity envieth not; charity vaunteth not itself, is not puffed up.

1 Corinthians 13:4

READ MATTHEW 5:9

Thankfulness

In every thing give thanks: for this is the will of God in Christ Jesus concerning you. ~1 Thessalonians 5:18

A THANKFUL MAN

Matthew Henry was walking down the street one day. Suddenly, some rough-looking men with straggly hair and dirty clothes appeared. Roughly they grabbed him, pulled his wallet out of his pocket, and ran off.

That evening Matthew was thinking about what had happened. He thought of the verse "In every thing give thanks." How could he be thankful when the robbers had taken his money?

He sat down to write in his diary, and he thought of four things to be thankful for:

1. I am thankful I was never robbed before.
2. They took all my money, but it wasn't much.
3. They didn't hurt me or take my life.
4. I am thankful I am not a robber.

We can always find things to grumble about, but if we look, we can always find good things to be thankful for.

We all like to be around thankful people, but who likes to be around a grumbler?

—You can grumble about the tangles in your hair.

    Or be thankful you have hair.

—You can grumble about washing the dishes.

    Or be thankful that you had food to make the dishes dirty.

—You can grumble about mowing the lawn.

    Or be thankful that you are strong and healthy.

—You can grumble that bees have stingers.

    Or be thankful that they make honey.

Sing more and watch the "grumbles" disappear.

Treasure Search

And let the peace of God rule in your hearts, to the which also ye are called in one body; and be ye thankful.

Let the word of Christ dwell in you richly in all wisdom; teaching and admonishing one another in psalms and hymns and spiritual songs, singing with grace in your hearts to the Lord.

And whatsoever ye do in word or deed, do all in the name of the Lord Jesus, giving thanks to God and the Father by him.

Colossians 3:15–17

READ PHILIPPIANS 2:14, 15

Good for Evil

But I say unto you which hear, Love your enemies, do good to them which hate you, Bless them that curse you, and pray for them which despitefully use you.
~Luke 6:27, 28

Sister Nancy was returning home from a good evening with friends. Happily she opened the gate and walked into her yard. Suddenly she stopped short and her mouth dropped open in shocked surprise. Her pretty flower beds were chopped down to the ground. Someone had ruined her flowers with a sharp machete. And then, they had picked up the prettiest flowers and strewn them in mock array on her sidewalk.

Who could have been so rude and mean? Sister Nancy felt sad and upset, but she remembered a piece of advice a friend had once shared, "When you are angry say, 'Praise the Lord' ten times; it will keep you from saying harsh words you will later regret."

Slowly she stooped to gather a lovely bouquet of the remains of her pretty flowers.

"Surely God would have me do something kind to whoever did this," Sister Nancy mused.

Later, one of Sister Nancy's good friends told her, "I know who chopped your flowers. It was my sister and her friend, and my sister has a birthday tomorrow."

"I know what I'll do," Sister Nancy said. "I'll cook a delicious birthday dinner for her, plus a chocolate cake." Sister Nancy got busy, frying chicken and stirring a delicious cake batter.

The next day, she took the birthday treat to the girls' home. As she neared the house, someone slipped out the back door and ran away.

The girls' mother answered her knock. "NO way!" the mother said when Sister Nancy explained why she had come. "You should not give them this dinner," she argued.

"Yes," said Sister Nancy, "I want to; I feel sorry for them. Something is wrong that they acted like that. I raked up the flowers; they will grow again, and here is a bouquet for your daughter too, from the flowers she cut."

Sister Nancy returned home with a light and happy heart. Her flowers were never bothered again.

What should you do when someone is rude to you?

Treasure Search

Therefore if thine enemy hunger, feed him; if he thirst, give him drink: for in so doing thou shalt heap coals of fire on his head.

Be not overcome of evil, but overcome evil with good.   Romans 12:20, 21

READ MATTHEW 5:44 AND LUKE 6:27, 28

What a Treasure

Love the Bible,
Read it each day;
This an act
That rich blessings will pay.

It shows how to live
In joy and in peace,
And crowns your life with goodness
That will never cease.

Take heed to God's Word;
Hold tight and hold fast
To its commandments and precepts,
That lead to heaven at last.

Order Form

To order, send this completed order form to:

Vision Publishers
P.O. Box 190
Harrisonburg, VA 22803
Fax: 540-437-1969
E-mail: orders@vision-publishers.com
www.vision-publishers.com

_____   _____
                     Name   Date

_____   _____
             Mailing Address   Phone

_____
             City   State   Zip

Light For Your Path   Qty. _____ x $10.99 each = _____
        (Please call for quantity discounts - 877-488-0901)

                                                            Price _____

                     Virginia residents add 5% sales tax _____

                 Ohio residents add applicable sales tax _____

                                     Shipping & handling __**$4.50**_____

                                            Grand Total _____

                                    All Payments in US Dollars

☐ Check #_____
☐ Money Order   ☐ Visa
☐ MasterCard   ☐ Discover

Name on Card _____

Card # __|__|__|__| __|__|__|__| __|__|__|__| __|__|__|__|

3-digit code from signature panel __|__|__| Exp. Date __|__|__|__|

Thank you for your order!

For a complete listing of our books write for our catalog.
Bookstore inquiries welcome

Order Form

To order, send this completed order form to:

Vision Publishers
P.O. Box 190
Harrisonburg, VA 22803
Fax: 540-437-1969
E-mail: orders@vision-publishers.com
www.vision-publishers.com

_____   _____
Name   Date

_____   _____
Mailing Address   Phone

_____   _____
City   State   Zip

Light For Your Path   Qty. ____ x $10.99 each = _____

(Please call for quantity discounts - 877-488-0901)

Price _____

Virginia residents add 5% sales tax _____

Ohio residents add applicable sales tax _____

Shipping & handling __$4.50__

Grand Total _____

All Payments in US Dollars

☐ Check #_____
☐ Money Order   ☐ Visa
☐ MasterCard   ☐ Discover

Name on Card _____

Card # _|__|__|__| _|__|__|__| _|__|__|__| _|__|__|__|

3-digit code from signature panel _|__|__| Exp. Date _|__|__|__|

Thank you for your order!

For a complete listing of our books write for our catalog.
Bookstore inquiries welcome

You Can Find Our Books at These Stores:

CALIFORNIA
Squaw Valley
Sequoia Christian Books
559/332-2606

COLORADO
Fruita
Grand Valley Dry Goods
970/858-1268

FLORIDA
Miami
Alpha and Omega
305/273-1263
Orlando
Borders Books and Music
407/826-8912

GEORGIA
Glennville
Vision Bookstore
912/654-4086
Montezuma
The Family Book Shop
478/472-5166

ILLINOIS
Arthur
Arthur Distributor Company
217/543-2166

Clearview Fabrics and Books
217/543-9091

Miller's Dry Goods
175-E County Road 50-N
Ava
Pineview Books
584 Bollman Road

INDIANA
Goshen
Miller's Country Store
574/642-3861

R And B's Kuntry Store
574/825-0191

Shady Walnut Grocery
574/862-2368
LaGrange
Pathway Bookstore
2580 North 250 West
Middlebury
F and L Country Store
574/825-7513

Laura's Fabrics
55140 County Road 43
Nappanee
Little Nook Bookstore
574/642-1347
Odon
Dutch Pantry
812/636-7922

Schrock's Kountry Korner
812/636-7842
Shipshewana
E and S Sales
260/768-4736
Wakarusa
Maranatha Christian Bookstore
574/862-4332

IOWA
Carson
Refining Fires Books
712/484-2214
Kalona
Friendship Bookstore
2357 540th Street SW

KANSAS
Hutchinson
Gospel Book Store
620/662-2875
Moundridge
Gospel Publishers
620/345-2532

**Our books may also be found on many
Choice Books bookracks and Lantern Books bookracks**

KENTUCKY
Manchester
  Lighthouse Ministries
  606/599-0607
Stephensport
  Martin's Bookstore
  270/547-4206

LOUISIANA
Belle Chasse
  Good News Bookstore
  504/394-3087

MARYLAND
Grantsville
  Shady Grove Market and
    Fabrics
  301/895-5660
Hagerstown
  J. Millers Gospel Store
  240/675-0383
Landover
  Integrity Church Bookstore
  301/322-3311
Oakland
  Countryside Books and More
  301/334-3318
Silver Spring
  Potomac Adventist Bookstore
  301/572-0700
Union Bridge
  Hege's Catalog Store
  410/775-7643

MICHIGAN
Burr Oak
  Chupp's Herbs and Fabric
  269/659-3950
Charlotte
  Meadow Ridge Woodcrafts
    LLC
  517/543-8680
Clare
  Colonville Country Store
  989/386-8686

Snover
  Country View Store
  989/635-3764

MISSOURI
Advance
  Troyer's Grocery
  573/722-3406
La Russell
  Schrock's Kountry Korner
  417/246-5351
Rutledge
  Zimmerman's Store
  660/883-5766
Seymour
  Byler Supply & Country Store
  417/935-4522
Shelbyville
  Windmill Ridge Bulk Foods
  4100 Highway T
Versailles
  Excelsior Bookstore
  573/378-1925
Weatherby
  Country Variety Store
  816/449-2932
Windsor
  Rural Windsor Books and
    Variety
  660/647-2705

NEW MEXICO
Farmington
  Lamp and Light Publishers
  505/632-3521

NEW YORK
Seneca Falls
  Sauder's Store
  315/568-2673

NORTH CAROLINA
Blanch
  Yoder's Country Market
  336/234-8072

**Our books may also be found on many
Choice Books bookracks and Lantern Books bookracks**

Greensboro
Borders Books and Music
336/218-0662
Raleigh
Borders Books and Music #365
919/755-9424

NORTH DAKOTA
Mylo
Lighthouse Bookstore
701/656-3331

OKLAHOMA
Miami
Eicher's Country Store
918/540-1871

OHIO
Berlin
Christian Aid Ministries
330/893-2428

Gospel Book Store
330/893-2523
Brinkhaven
Little Cottage Books
740/824-3808
Dalton
Little Country Store
330/828-8411
Fredricksburg
Faith-View Books
330/674-4129
Leetonia
Tinkling Spring Country Store
330/482-4592
Mesopotamia
Eli Miller's Leather Shop
440/693-4448
Middlefield
S & E Country Store
440/548-2347
Millersburg
Country Furniture & Bookstore
330/893-4455

Plain City
Deeper Life Bookstore
614/873-1199
Seaman
Keim Family Market
937/386-9995
Sugarcreek
JSR Fabric and Shoes
330/852-2721

The Gospel Shop
330/852-4223

Troyer's Bargain Store
2101 County Road 70

OREGON
Estacada
Bechtel Books
530/630-4606
Halsey
Shoppe of Shalom
541/369-2369

PENNSYLVANIA
Amberson
Scroll Publishing Co.
717/349-7033
Belleville
Yoder's Gospel Book Store
717/483-6697
Chambersburg
Burkholder Fabrics
717/369-3155

Pearson's Pasttimes
717/267-1415
Denver
Weaver's Store
717/445-6791
Ephrata
Clay Book Store
717/733-7253

Conestoga Bookstore
717/354-0475

**Our books may also be found on many
Choice Books bookracks and Lantern Books bookracks**

Home Messenger Library &
Bookstore
717/351-0218

Ken's Educational Joys
717/351-8347

Gordonville
Ridgeview Bookstore
717/768-7484

Greencastle
Country Dry Goods
717/593-9661

Guys Mills
Christian Learning Resource
814/789-4769

Leola
Conestoga Valley Bookbindery
717/656-8824

Lewisburg
Crossroads Gift and Bookstore
570/522-0536

McVeytown
Penn Valley Christian Retreat
717/899-5000

Meadville
Gingerich Books and Notions
814/425-2835

Monroe
Border's Books and Music
412/374-9772

Mount Joy
Mummau's Christian Bookstore
717/653-6112

Myerstown
Witmer's Clothing
717/866-6845

Newville
Corner Store
717/776-4336

Rocky View Bookstore
717/776-7987

Parkesburg
Brookside Bookstore
717/692-4759

Quarryville
Countryside Bargains
717/528-2360

Shippensburg
Mt. Rock Bookstore
717/530-5726

Springboro
Chupp's Country Cupboard
814/587-3678

SOUTH CAROLINA
Barnwell
The Genesis Store
803/541-6109

North Charleston
World Harvest Ministries
843/554-7960

Summerville
Manna Christian Bookstore
843/873-4221

Sumter
Anointed Word Christian
Bookstore
803/494-9894

TENNESSEE
Crossville
MZL English Book Ministry
931/277-3686

Troyer's Country Cupboard
931/277-5886

Deer Lodge
Mt. Zion Literature Ministry
931/863-8183

Paris
Miller's Country Store
731/644-7535

Sparta
Valley View Country Store
931/738-5465

TEXAS
Kemp
Heritage Market and Bakery
903/498-3366

**Our books may also be found on many
Choice Books bookracks and Lantern Books bookracks**

Seminole
Nancy's Country Store
432/758-9162

VIRGINIA
Bristow
The Lighthouse Books
703/530-9039
Dayton
Books of Merit
540/879-2628

Mole Hill Books & More
540/867-5928

Rocky Cedars Enterprises
540/879-9714
Harrisonburg
Christian Light Publications
540/434-0768
McDowell
Sugar Tree Country Store
540/396-3469
Rural Retreat
Bender's Fabrics
276/686-4793
Woodbridge
Mennonite Maidens
703/622-3018

WASHINGTON
North Bonneville
Moore Foundation
800/891-5255

WEST VIRGINIA
Renick
Yoders' Select Books
304/497-3990

WISCONSIN
Dalton
Mishler's Country Store
West 5115 Barry Rd.
Granton
Mayflower Country Store
715/238-7988

South Wayne
Pilgrim's Pantry
608/439-1064

CANADA

BRITISH COLUMBIA
Burns Lake
Wildwood Bibles and Books
250/698-7451
Montney
Janice Martin Books
250/327-3231

MANITOBA
Arborg
Sunshine Christian Books
204/364-3135

ONTARIO
Aylmer
Mennomex
519/773-2002
Brunner
Country Cousins
519/595-4277

Lighthouse Books
519/595-4500
Floradale
Hillcrest Home Baking and
Dry Goods
519/669-1381
Linwood
Living Waters Christian Book-
store
519/698-1198
Mount Forest
Shady Lawn Books
519/323-2830
Newton
Canadian Family Resources
519/595-7585

**Our books may also be found on many
Choice Books bookracks and Lantern Books bookracks**